BELLA DONNA

RAY MILLS

Fulton Books
Meadville, PA

Published by Fulton Books 2022

ISBN 979-8-88505-317-4 (paperback)
ISBN 979-8-88505-318-1 (digital)

Printed in the United States of America

I'm Ramon Molina. The fifteenth birthday is a huge event in my culture. When a young boy turns fifteen, he is a *man*. On my fifteenth birthday, I encountered a man that changed my life forever and took me on an adventure like few boys my age would ever encounter. An adventure on the high seas. An adventure of danger, love, and family.

This is my story, Ramon Molina.

CHAPTER I

HAPPY BIRTHDAY

It was early morning. I lay in bed listening to the early-morning sounds coming from the jungle. A big male howler monkey was claiming his domain. I could smell the smoke from the other *casitas* cooking with carbon wood. Suddenly, I remembered. *Finally, I'm a man. Today is my fifteenth birthday.*

I knew I wouldn't receive a big birthday gift. I wasn't expecting one. I also knew my mom would make me a nice breakfast, and my sister would give me a big smile and a day off from her usual teasing.

I heard my mom tinkering out back in the kitchen, and I smiled at the thought of Salchichas, egg, beans, and tortillas. I stumbled outside to the kitchen pretending to be half asleep. The typical cooking area was outside the house underneath a roof but open and usually surrounded by a short wall.

My mom was average in height. Brown eyes and brown hair. I thought she was the prettiest woman in San German. She was quiet with a pleasant smile and seemed to love everyone and everything, animals, children, flowers—everything.

I walked up to my mom and gave her a quick kiss on the cheek. She looked at me, "When it is light enough to see, I need you to go to town and buy some flour and meal. Tell Mr. Martin I will pay him soon."

My blood went to my head. I was suddenly really upset. *No, happy birthday, Ramon. No, I love you, my young caballero. Nothing but demands for me to go to town and buy groceries. Woman's work! She could have sent Rena!* Such were my thoughts as I walked down the mountain towards town, on the biggest day of my life.

My hometown or village would be more correct, was called San German. It was named after a pirate that established the town with the money he had gained in his adventures on the sea. I didn't really believe the story and never understood how the church would claim a pirate to be a saint. San German was on the edge of the sea with mountains behind the town.

There were rumors that there were Islands further out to sea and if you went west for many days there was a land so big that no one knew if it had an end. This place was called America. There were all kinds of people that lived in America. Some said they were evil and ate other people. Some said they were demons and rarely took baths or swam to clean up for supper. One thing I knew, I was perfectly happy in San German.

As I neared the town, I began to see more people. The rainy season was over, so it was pleasant. I passed Guiermo, a rugged man I knew from the mountain. Most people were afraid of him. Some called him Diablo or devil. He was always friendly to me. Guiermo was leading a burro loaded with coffee beans.

"You going to see the big ship that came into port two days ago," he asked excitedly. "A two-mast with four sails."

"I didn't know about it," I replied. I could feel excitement swelling up inside. *No ship that size had ever come into San German's harbor.* "What kind of ship is it? Cargo?"

Guiermo smiled, "Cargo? Are you kidding? That is a pirate ship for sure. As soon as I deliver these coffee beans, I'm going to get a better look. What about you?"

"It could be both, cargo and pirate!" After a pause for thinking, I decided against it. "I better not go look at it. My mom is waiting for me to bring back some flour and meal from town. Today's my birthday, and I think she wants to make something special."

Guiermo placed his hand on my shoulder. "You turned fifteen today? Is your dad going to take you to visit with Meme? She will make a man out of you."

Meme was a local prostitute and every young male in San German knew who and what she was. Immediately Guiermo was sorry he said that. I could see the embarrassment on his face.

"I'm sorry," he said. "I was just excited."

"That's okay. I better get going." As I walked down the hill, I felt more like I should have stayed in bed. My birthday was not going well at all. Apparently, my mom forgot it was my birthday. Guiermo just reminded me, it was a tradition that the father would take the son to a local prostitute on the night of his fifteenth birthday and she would, "Make a man out of him."

Although I thought about it, I shoved the thought into the back of my mind. I really wasn't concerned that I would not have that experience, I just wished my father could have been here.

I didn't dwell on the matter. My Father had not been seen since I was five years old. He went into town for a meeting of the leaders of San German and to drink with some friends. He never came back.

My mother never remarried, and often I would see her sitting in the yard looking out to sea as if waiting for him to come home again. Once at night, there was a beautiful moon and she asked me, "Do you think your father can see the same moon tonight?"

"Maybe," I saw a tear in her eye and said, "I think he can, and he is thinking the same as you."

I arrived at the tienda belonging to Mr. Martin. It was just a small building with a roof and three walls. At night he simply hung a rope across the front, and everyone knew he was close. No one ever stole anything but would sometimes leave money in a basket. No one ever took the basket.

"Good morning, Ramon," he said with a huge smile, his white teeth showing beneath a gray bushy mustache. "What brings you down from the mountain?"

"My mother sent me to get flour and meal. She said she will pay you soon."

"Of course, she will. How are your mother and sister?"

"They're good."

He gave me a quizzical look, "You don't seem like you feel ok. Are you sick?"

"*No*," I replied. "It's just that…," and I cut myself off and was sure he could tell I was a little choked up. My sadness suddenly turned to frustration. *I'm a man, and men don't show their emotions so easily.*

He wiped his hands on a white cloth. "Ramon, I can see you're upset about something." He began filling two sacks. One with meal and the other with flour, "I've known you since your birth. I will not pry into your business, but you seem upset. Is it something I said that offends you?"

"No, sir," I replied. Wishing to change the subject I asked, "Have you seen the ship that came into port two days ago?"

"Yes. It is a big one. A brigantine, I think," he squinted his eyes, "I think maybe she has twelve guns at least. I don't think she is military, so I ask myself, what kind of ship would have so many gun portals? I can only think of one kind." He looked at me with huge eyes. "Pirates!"

That startled me a little, and yet it made me excited as well. "Pirates? Well, shouldn't someone find out? What if they attack San German?"

He shrugged his shoulders, "Maybe they just want fresh water and supplies? I certainly will not refuse to sell to them what they ask. A pirate's money is still money. By the way." He walked to the counter.

"I have something for you. It's not much but," and he produced a huge piece of chocolate bar covered in coconut. "I believe today is a special day for you," he said with a smile.

A huge smile came to my face. *Someone remembered my birthday.* I took the gift, said thank you, and walked away only to immediately return for the flour and meal.

"Excuse me, gentlemen." A man seemed to appear from thin air. He was a tall dark man. He was dressed in black breeches with a white shirt and a red sash around his waist. In that sash were two pistols and a sword.

"I did not intend to startle you. I overheard your conversation. Allow me to introduce myself. I am Pablo Sanchez Goma of Brazil," he said with pride.

"I am first mate to Capitan Luis De Gaza. The beautiful lady anchored in your harbor is the *Bella Donna*. I come to you for two reasons. We are indeed in need of supplies and freshwater."

He looked at me eye to eye, "Reason number two. The *capitan* is in need of a cabin boy to tend his cabin and run errands on the ship. Delivering messages, helping the cook, and such." He looked down at me. He arched his eyebrow. "Are you employed, young man?"

I swallowed hard, "Me, sir?" I could hardly speak, and my question sounded more like a whisper.

He gave me a big smile from a thin mustache, "Of course, you. The gentleman is much too elder to be a cabin boy."

Mr. Martin cleared his throat. "Do forgive my intrusion, good sir? If you will be so kind as to give me a list of your request, I will be glad to fill it for you."

Mr. Goma, without moving his head, looked at Mr. Sanchez rather seriously, then suddenly smiled, "Of course, the list. I was caught up with the young man." Gesturing with his hands, "Imagining him on the high seas with the wind in his hair." He pointed to the west and moved his hand in an ocean wave motion, "Sailing towards the sunset in search of adventure like no other." Ending the motion, with his hands making a wide circle.

He reached inside his shirt and retrieved a list of items, "If you need some assistance with the words, I will help you. I can speak Spanish, English, and French, but can only write in Portuguese."

I was indeed caught up in my own imagination much as he described. *He called me a man.* The other thing I was thinking was, *How much money can I earn, and how in the world can I ask my mother for permission?*

"But can only write in Portuguese," he was saying. "Excuse me, sir. How much money would a cabin boy make?"

"Ah, so you are interested. Tell me. What is your name young man?"

He called me a man again. "My name is Donaldo Ramon Molina. I'm from here in San German." I immediately felt silly adding the last part. He looked at me and seemed to turn a shade lighter in color.

"Very well. Do you prefer Donaldo or Ramon?"

"Ramon."

"In two days, we will set sail. Be at the long peer before sunrise in two days, and the job will be yours. Now if you will excuse me, I have a very important matter I need to attend." He spun around sharply and began to walk away.

I ran after him, "Sir Goma! Wait, please. I have a question for you."

He stopped and turned around, "Yes?"

"What happened to the last cabin boy?"

He looked at me seriously and said, "He grew up. We didn't eat him." He turned away and walked towards the long pier.

On the pier there were large baskets and small pens with chickens and ducks stacked to be loaded onto the *Bella Donna*. Shallow longboats were going to and from the *Bella Donna* to the long pier. One even had a cow in it. The boats came to the pier empty and returned loaded with supplies.

It was midmorning. I knew my mother was worried and angry at the same time. I imagined she would have been finished with her plans for the flour and meal. I began my climb back up the mountain road towards my home. I had all sorts of things going through my mind. *How long will I be gone? The last cabin boy grew up! What did he mean, "We didn't eat him?" Was he from America? He appeared dark skin. The stories say the people from America are white. Where is Brazil?* Suddenly my world seemed so much smaller.

When I arrived home, my mom met me in the front yard, and I was correct. My mom was really upset, "*Hijo*, where have you been? I have been worried sick about you. Did you get the flour and the meal?"

She wiped the sweat from her forehead, "Ave Maria! What took you so long? I need the flour to make tortillas and *pan*." She took the flour and meal and went around the back of the house where she cooked.

I was without words. She still didn't say anything about my birthday, and she needs the flour and meal for tortillas and pan. *Nothing special!*

The kitchen was traditional, a fire pit made of stone and plaster with a metal grate over the top. The metal grate is what she cooked on. In the corner was another fire pit that was round with a mall door. She used this for baking.

Rena, my sister, came outside. She was younger than me by two years. Most people thought she was older than me. I could never figure that out.

Rena placed her hands on her hips, "Wow! Mom was worried about you. You should never have been gone that long. What on earth were you doing? Talking to Linda again?"

Linda was a girl I had a crush on since I could remember, "You know better than that. We are just friends. I could marry her tomorrow if I wanted to."

"Are you stupid? You're just a kid."

"I am not! Today I am fifteen years old. That makes me a man."

"You were a kid yesterday, and today you are a man? What changed when you were sleeping?"

"I did. I am fifteen now."

Rena tilted her head to one side, "So, Mr. Ramon, get a job if you're a man. Linda probably would marry you. She likes you a lot. That's why when she says goodbye, she hugs you two or three times. She wants you to kiss her. How a man kisses is very important to a woman. Stupid."

"You don't know what you're talking about. Go find someone else to bother."

It's my birthday, and she still didn't say happy birthday or anything.

I walked around the house to where my mom was making the tortillas. She was making a lot because she sold or traded them and made them for us to eat as well.

I sat on the wall trying to work up the courage to ask for permission to take the cabin boy job. *Just blurt it out.*

"I think I would like to go to work to earn money," I said. My mom glanced at me to see if she really heard me correctly. "Yes, I would like to find a job on a boat. I could learn how to be a deckhand or something."

She began padding a tortilla from one hand to the other, "If you are serious, why not start on a fishing boat? Something small. In a few years, when you are older you can move up to larger ships."

"I'm old enough and big enough now. Why wait until I'm older?"

"Ramon, I still need you here every day. You're still my child, and I would worry every day if you left out to sea on some merchant ship. You are still too young. They want men to work on the ships. You are still a child."

I was becoming frustrated. My mom just called me a child and said I was too young to work on a ship.

"I have you know I met a man in town today. That's what took me so long. He offered me a job as a cabin boy on a ship. It's a big ship. Mr. Martin said it is a brigantine ship. They are here to pick up supplies." My mom stopped padding the tortillas. I continued, "This man is the first mate to the captain. He thought I would make a good captain's boy."

My mom was facing me now, "What is the name of this ship, or did the kind gentlemen tell you that?" She was suddenly, visibly concerned. "Did anyone follow you home?"

"*No.*"

"Are you sure, Ramon?"

"Yes, Mom, I'm sure. Why?'

My mom began to pace and look towards the sea, "Who else saw this man?"

"Mr. Martin. He was in the store. We all talked. The man's name was Sanchez Goma of Brazil. He seemed like a very nice man and well dressed." I paused, "Mom! I knew you would be upset, but what is going on?"

The sun was going down, and the howler monkeys were at it again. I really liked to hear them but not too closely.

My mom looked at me seriously, "You can't trust everyone you meet in life. Sometimes when the big ships come to port, there are people taken in the middle of the night, and no one ever hears from them again. Did the stranger happen to mention the name of his ship?"

"The *Bella Donna*!"

My mom suddenly sat on the wall surrounding the kitchen. She was pale. Her hands were shaking. Her eyes teared up, "That is the ship…that was in port when your father disappeared."

I couldn't believe what I just heard. So many things were going through my mind I couldn't form a word. I sat down on the wall.

My mom stood with a look of sadness, yet defiant, "I have waited all these years for that ship to come back to port hoping my husband would come home with that ship. Now the *Bella Donna* is back and without your father." She started crying harder, "I fear him dead."

I walked over to my mother, grabbed her, and held her tight, "Mom! I'm so sorry! I had no idea." I began to cry. *What have I done?* I turned from my mother and ran into the darkness towards the road. There was a huge Guanacaste tree. I sat down and leaned against the tree, sobbing. I never saw my mom cry like that. It was as if I broke her heart. I hated myself!

I heard Rena yell out, "What did you do, Ramon Molina?"

I don't know how long I sat there staring out over the jungle at the sea. A thought began to form. *Someone on that ship knew about my father.* I was more determined to get that job and find out. *I will bring my father home if he is still alive. If he left by his choice, I will kill him.* Late in the night I crept back into the house. *Tomorrow I will reveal my plan to Mom. She will still be upset. But I will leave with that ship!*

I tossed and turned all night. The next morning, I found my mom in the kitchen as usual. I gave her a hug, a little longer than I would have normally. She handed me a plate of beans and an egg with a couple of tortillas. She said nothing. I sat down and began eating.

"That may be the last good meal you eat in a long time," she said, with her back to me. "I hear the food on the ships is close to ruined and not fit to give to a pig."

I looked at my mom. I could sense a little frustration in her voice. I put down my plate, "How did you know I was going to talk to you again about that job?"

She turned and faced me. "Because you are just like your father, hardheaded. Hard as a coconut!"

"Mom, someone on that ship knows my father. Your husband." I stiffened my back. I'm going to find out where he is or where he was killed. I'm going to bring him home if he is alive. I paused. If he is alive and does not wish to come home? Well…"

Mom looked at me as if she saw me for the first time, "My young man, I cannot stop you from sailing away on that ship. I hate that the *Bella Donna* came back. I have watched and waited for ten years thinking, hoping, she would bring your father back."

She turned away from me, "Now, she is taking you too. It's almost more than I can bear. But I will not stand in your way." She walked over, placed her hands on my face, and kissed my forehead. She then walked back into the house. I sat there in the kitchen for a while longer trying to wrap my head around what was taking place.

The remainder of the day I spent with Rena and Mom. It was solemn though. Rena tried to play it off and encouraged me to get my few things ready to take with me. It wasn't much. A change of clothing. A small knife. A bar of soap.

My mom came into the room holding some paper rolled up with a piece of yarn binding the roll. She handed it to me, "I don't have anything for you to write with. If you find something, or maybe someone will have something, you can use it to keep a journal. When you return, we can read the journal and you can tell us your adventures. Maybe draw some things you find interesting…" and Mom began to cry a little more.

"I will!" I really did not know what to say, and the night was turning into the morning.

I made my farewells. I picked up my swag and started down the hill towards the pier. Just out of the glow from the lantern in the house, I stopped, turned around, and stared for a minute. I felt the tears swelling up inside. *This may be the last time I see my house for a very long time. Father in heaven, please take care of my mother and sister. Bring me back home safe and soon!* I turned and continued towards the harbor. The closer I got to the pier the sadness began to be replaced with excitement.

I was walking towards the few remaining crates stacked on the pier. At the end of the pier were three men talking and smoking. I could see their faces in the glow when they puffed their pipe. A boat was tied at the end of the pier. As I was passing the crates, a skinny man slightly hunched in the shoulders, stepped from between the crates into my path, "SSStand fast. Who might you be? SState your name boy!"

I stepped back. The man's voice was soft and low. When he pronounced *S*, it was drawn out. *This man sounds like a snake!* I found myself slowly trying to find my knife. My mom used to say, "When a person gets frightened, they will run or fight.

It usually depends on the person and their experience in life." The seconds between his question and my answer seemed like forever.

"Are you daft, boy? Ssstate your name!"

"My name is Ramon Molina, sir."

"He is no sir, Ramon. Scallywag is more like it. Snake, leave the boy be! This is the new cabin boy. The captain's boy." The man speaking was Sanchez Goma, the man from the tienda. "I see you have taken the offer."

Snake interrupted, "I was just messing around SSSanchez. We best ssshove off. *Capitan* will be wanting to weigh anchor in a bit." Snake turned and walked towards the boat at the end of the pier.

"Yes, sir," I replied. "I am willing to learn all I can. I turned fifteen two days ago. I want to earn all the money I can." I was looking up at him with a proud face and my chest out.

His face glowed once again from his pipe. "What will you do with all the money you make?"

"I will build my mother a big house overlooking the ocean. She will never have to sell tortillas or work again."

Sanchez drew on his pipe again, "First we must get the money. Yes? We better go now. The *capitan*, he waits for us."

As we rowed to the ship, I reached for an ore to help. "No!" Snake said without turning around. The captain's boy does not row." He never looked at me. I wasn't sure how he knew I was reaching for the ore.

It was getting lighter, and I could see the *Bella Donna* more clearly. She seemed to get bigger as we got closer. I could hear men talking and the occasional thump or clanging metal. On the upper deck of the fortress, I could see a dark figure of a man standing looking in our direction. There were several rope ladders hanging on the side of the ship. We pulled up to one of these, and two ropes came splashing into the water. Snake and another man tied a rope to iron hoops on each end of the small boat.

"Up the ladder you go, Ramon," said Snake.

I grabbed my swag and scampered up the ladder trying not to appear too clumsy. I reached the top and a huge hand grabbed me by my arm and before I knew it, I was on the deck facing a huge black man. He had a big smile with bright teeth.

"Welcome aboard," he said in a very strong accent. "My name is Vincent. I will assist you." He hesitated as he looked around at the crew and raised his voice a little and then continued. "The captain said for me to help you in all things. I always obey the captain." He spoke to me but was looking at everyone else.

I looked around but did not see anyone who might be a captain. It was early daylight, and I could see fine.

I looked towards the upper deck of the fortress but saw no one there. The crowd started to separate with everyone going about their chores and seemed to have lost interest in me.

"Come," said Vincent. "I will show you your quarters."

We climbed the stairs and entered the Fortress. This was the name given to the first, second, and third decks behind the mainmast. The captain's quarter was on the third deck. We walked along the narrow side. Only a rope to keep you from falling over. Some fancier ships had railings along the walk.

As we climbed the walkway I stopped and looked back at shore. I couldn't help but wonder how long it would be before I saw the shore again.

"You coming?" asked Vincent.

I turned and walked the rest of the way. From the third deck I could see the Guanacaste tree my father and I use to sit beneath. I was only five. I couldn't remember his face, but I could remember those times shared with him beneath that big tree. It appeared even bigger from here.

CHAPTER II

BELLA DONNA

We entered a small cabin. To one side was a hammock. "This is your quarters. You may open the window if you like. The door there," he gestured with a nod of his head, "enters the captain's quarter. Only open that door if this bell rings." Beside the door was a small bell with a string attached.

Vincent turned to leave but turned around and gave me serious look, "Don't go wandering around the ship at night. Not everyone is trustworthy. The ship's cook will be expecting you. Don't make him send for you!" Vincent disappeared from the doorway. I threw my swag onto the hammock and left in search of the kitchen.

I asked the first man I saw where I could find the kitchen. He was a thinly built man with flat hair and a white bandana around his head. He had a nasty-looking scar down the left cheek, just behind the eye from cheek to chin. He smiled at my question, "There is no kitchen on this ship. But if it's the galley you're looking for, it is below your feet."

I started down the stairs when the ship suddenly lurched forward, "Row you noodle arm dandies. Put your back into it," came a loud voice below deck. "Row I say!" I peered over the edge and saw ores from fore to aft rowing in unison. The sails were still wrapped tightly in their places.

I found the galley. A short round man with a kind round face met me at the door.

"Are you the stowaway or the captain's boy?" he asked.

"The cabin boy?" I repeated. I have never met the captain, and I am not his boy."

"Ah, but you are." He motioned me into the galley, "You mind your manners around the captain. You might survive to return home someday. Grab a knife and start peeling those spuds. Save the peels they make a strong drink!"

I selected a small knife and began peeling potatoes. I looked around the galley. There were several knives hanging on the wall. Hanging from the ceiling and swaying with the motion of the ship were several pots and pans. I decided not to look at them too long, the swaying made me a little queasy. Roasting over a pit made of stone and iron was a slab of meat that appeared to be beef. The smell was great! The cook went about his business.

It was mid-morning. I could feel the ship gently rise and fall. I could hear the sails flapping in the wind. I had long since completed my task of peeling potatoes. I didn't really know what else to do. I asked, "Is there anything else?"

"My name is Roberto. You never answered my question. I've been waiting all morning for you to answer my question. Are you the stowaway?"

"No. I'm not. My name is Ramon. Is there a stowaway?"

"He thinks he is, but everyone knows he is here. Someone will come across him."

"What will happen to him?"

"The captain will decide. He could dance the hempen jig. I say put him to work. That's one less person we must shanghai. We are still shorthanded."

"Dance the hempen jig? You mean to hang him?"

"That's right, boy. If he is able-bodied, he won't likely dance the hempen jig."

"Shanghai? You mean kidnap," I said, surprised to hear someone admit to such a thing.

Roberto drew on his pipe. "Well, now those are some harsh words! I need not use such a palaver! Kidnap." he said disgustingly.

I sat up straight, "When you *shanghai* someone, are they willing to come along?"

"Well of course not! You put something in their drink, they pass out and wake up out to sea. It's not like we wait in the dark and bonk them on the head!" He took a deep breath. "Were decent folk here on the *Bella Donna*," said Roberto, with a look of bewilderment.

I could not believe my ears. "If the person had no choice, he was kidnapped!" I blurted out.

"Tit for tat, says I. It's all in how you look at it," said Roberto.

Just short of mid-day Roberto, myself, and two other hands carved up the meat and placed it in a large black pot. The potatoes were boiled. Slices of bread were placed in other pots. These pots were carried below deck and the crew ate under the watchful eye of the first mate. He was ensuring that no one got more than their share, and everyone had something to eat.

"No one eats a bite until everyone has theirs," he said. There was a rumbling of contest to this command, but no one dared as much as taste a sample. Such was every meal taken on board the *Bella Donna*.

"The captains waiting for his," said Roberto. "Come along! I'll show you the ropes, so you don't flub it up."

We returned to the galley where Roberto had put aside three dishes. I expected the captain's plate to be fancy, maybe even gold plates. His plate was no different than ours. Metal plates and cups. Everything used by the captain was common for the crew.

"Place the plate by the door of the captain's quarter, ring the bell, and leave. Do not attempt to look at him. He will present himself to you when he is ready to do so. He hates a sneak." He grabbed my ear. "You hearing me, boy?"

Wincing at the pain I replied, "I hear you, sir!" I rubbed my ear and walked to the door to the captain's quarter. As instructed, I placed the plate on a small stool beside the door. I gave the bell three good jerks on the string and ran out of the room. I stopped just outside my door but out of sight. I waited for what seemed like an hour. I never heard a single noise.

I finally reentered the room as if I were looking for something but was scared to even look towards the plate. Finally, I gave the plate a glance. The plate was empty and appeared to have been cleaned.

Several days had passed. I still had not mentioned my father. It was clear that they would often take a person in the night and that person would awaken at sea with no way of getting back. I had taken to walking around the deck at night, even though I had been advised against it. It was dark one night, no moon at all. I had made my way to the foremast and was hunkered down in some rope and gaff sail. I was about to fall asleep when I heard three voices approaching, talking in a hushed tone. One of the men was Snake. There was no mistaking his voice and the way he pronounced words.

"I sssay we cut his throat and be done with the rat."

"Don't be too quick. It won't be that easy. We will have to kill all of them," said another voice. I thought this might be Goma of Brazil.

Someone else was speaking. "I found him in the bilge below the hold. I heard something and went to investigate. There he was. Crawling around on all fours like he enjoyed being there." I was sure this voice was that of Pablo the friendly. He didn't seem too friendly. He always had a look about him that suggested he didn't like anyone.

I was suddenly worried. I was about to be caught and killed. They had found the one for which they were searching. *Was it the stowaway? They were going to kill them all. They had agreed on that.* I remained motionless, listening as they continued their planning.

"There! That wasn't too hard. SSSSee. Dead."

Pablo sighed, "Throw it overboard. We can kill the others, another night."

I heard a small splash, "I hate rats," said Pablo.

I breathed a sigh of relief. *It was really a rat. Not a person.* I remained where I was until I was sure no one else was around and returned to my quarter.

It was braking day the next morning. We were about to deliver the breakfast to the crew. Suddenly there was a shout from the watchman in the crow's nest. "Hoay! Sails to the port side. Sails to the port side!" The ship was suddenly bustling with men shouting commands and running here and there. Some were brandishing weapons. Suddenly there was a shrill whistle. "Captain on deck," someone shouted. Everyone stopped in their tracks and looked towards the fortress. I turned and looked as well. There was the captain dressed in all black with a red sash around his waist. There were at least three pistols in his sash. A curved sword hung on his left hip. Slung across his shoulder was a shotgun, bigger than a pistol but shorter than a common long gun. His complexion was dark. He was well-groomed with long black hair and a thin mustache.

CHAPTER III

JOHN DAVID NAU

I looked to the east, and there were several sails. I counted eight ships. Their sails had markings I did not recognize. They weren't from Spain or Portugal.

"Run up the white," said the captain.

"Run up the white, "shouted Goma the first mate. A man hoisted a large white flag to the top of the mainmast.

The captain turned and faced the men, "Close the gun ports. Do not secure them. Place your weapons out of sight, but keep them handy." The captain said all this and his voice carried, but he never raised his voice or showed emotion.

"Come here, boy," he said without looking. Without hesitation I scampered to the upper deck of the fortress and presented myself to the captain. He handed me a brass spyglass, "Tell me what you see."

I placed the spyglass to my eye. "Adjust the view by sliding this," and he placed my hand on the largest part of the tube and slid it back towards my eye. I then repeated the motion until the view became clear. I jerked my head away. *How is that possible?* The ships were still a long way away but closing fast. When I looked in the glass, they were almost close enough to touch.

"What do you see?" he asked again.

"I see eight ships. Each ship seems to have a large crew." I described the flag.

"That is the fleet of Jon David Nau. The flag he flies is that of France. Captain Nau has eight ships and four hundred men." The men began to chatter among themselves, clearly uneasy.

"We can outrun them, sir!" said Goma. "Just say the word! We will run up the gaffs."

The captain looked at me, "Captain Nau has a nasty way of torturing his enemies. He is widely known for being extremely cruel. Captain seized the towns of Gibraltar and Maracaibo of Venezuela. He especially hates Spain."

First Mate Goma said again, "We can outrun him!"

The captain looked at me, I thought I saw a glimmer of a smile. He arched his eyebrow, "We are not Spain, and he knows me. We will host him for breakfast in my quarters. Run along and tell Roberto to assist in the preparations for the morning meal. Nothing Spanish!" He turned, overlooking the crew below. "Keep steady. Be courteous but aware at all times!"

"Nothing Spanish," grumbled Roberto. "What are we supposed to serve a Frenchman? We have no snails!" Roberto was clearly upset. He cooked up eggs, bacon, potatoes, and some kind of bread. "That's the last of my eggs. I was saving them," grumbled Roberto.

"For what," I asked.

"For something! Anything more special than this!"

While this was cooking. We went upstairs to the captain's quarters. There was a large round table in the center of the room. A simple hammock was slung in one corner, a smaller square table in front of shelves loaded with books and charts. In the opposite corner was a cell made of steel bars. At the stern was a large window that nearly spanned the entire wall.

"Speak nothing of what you see in this room, Ramon! Nothing," Roberto said.

"I won't, sir," I replied. Roberto hastily left the room and returned to the galley.

Captain Nau boarded the *Bella Donna* without pomp and circumstance. It appeared he was pleased to be aboard the *Bella Donna*. He greeted Capitan Luis De Gaza as if they were best friends that hadn't seen each other for a long time. We served the captains their breakfast.

"You must let me bring your cook with me when I leave," said Captain Nau.

"I'm afraid that is impossible," said Captain Gaza. "I could never replace him. A good cook is an answer to keeping a crew in good spirit. If you don't have a good cook, you must have a good supply of rum." The two men laughed and continued in the conversation for hours.

I was just outside of the captain's door in my quarters waiting to answer any request that might be made of me. Their conversation was about past raids in Venezuela. A place called Vieques, Puerto Rico, and the list went on. I began to think. *The captain used to sail with Captain Nau. They were old acquaintances. Maybe that explains the cell in the captain's quarters. The captain likes to torture captured enemies as well.* I was beginning to get a good picture of this captain. I had only just met the man and already he seemed like a very polite, killer of men. *We didn't eat him,* Goma had said the day I met him when I asked what had happened to the last captain's boy. I was becoming a little uneasy. I remained next to the tiny bell in my room. I could not hear their conversation, only muffled voices and an occasional laugh.

Captain Nau asked Captain Gaza, "Who is the young lad? It seems I should know him."

Captain Gaza smiled, "He is the son of a dear friend of ours."

Captain Nau tilted his head back and smiled. "You mean he is the son of Reynaldo Molina?"

"Yes," Gaza replied. "No other."

"The same Reynaldo 'The Judge,' Molina," asked Captain Nau. " I thought as much. He looks just like him. But surely he is not alive. He was captured by the Turks." Captain Nau lifted his hand in a gesture of unbelief, "He was either killed or sold into slavery. I'm sure of it," said Captain Nau, a little bewildered.

Captain Gaza walked to the huge window gazing aft, "Last year we took a supposed merchant ship laden with slaves bound for Puerto Rico and Port Royal. The slaves were to be sold to the Dutch." Captain

Gaza turned and faced Captain Nau, "There was a captive. When I asked where he was from, he said they were taken off the coast of the Barbary and held captive in a Turkish prison called Cafa. He stated there was a man there that was speaking the same language as me and he called himself Reynaldo. His description was that of Reynaldo. He stated that Reynaldo was a prisoner, but he had won favor with the Turks because he was ruthless but very intelligent and learned their language quickly. They gave him leave, but he was not free. He helped maintain their books and such."

Captain Nau joined him at the window, "So, you intend to go get him?"

"Yes, I intend to go get him."

Just before noon, Captain Nau departed the *Bella Donna*. The two captains clasped hands.

"Don't forget to keep an eye out for Calico Jack. Since Captain Vane accepted his pardon, Jack is running around with two wenches. One of which is Ann Bonnie," said Captain Nau. He stepped onto the Jacob's ladder to go down to his longboat.

"That is bad news. Those two together are quite ruthless," replied Captain Gaza.

Captain Nau paused on the third rung and looked up, "Are you sure you don't want to join my fleet? We can use you."

Captain Gaza smiled and slightly shook his head yes and replied, "No. I enjoy my freedom. I have an adventure awaiting me of the Barbary. Nothing can sway what lies ahead of me."

With that, Captain Nau was on his way back to his fleet. "If you change your mind," he yelled back. "I will be off the coast of Venezuela for the next few months."

The next couple of weeks passed without excitement. I decided I was going to look for this stowaway that was supposed to be somewhere on this ship. I decided I would check in the hold first. It seemed like some of the fruit and brined vegetables were disappearing faster than they should be.

The code on the *Bella Donna* stated that no one eats more than their portion. I went to the hold and lit a candle for light. There didn't seem to be anywhere a person could hide. We had been at sea for weeks. No one had found anyone that was not supposed to be here. Everything was tied down in neat stacks. There was no place a person could hide here in the hold. I had searched everywhere I could think of a person might hide. Everywhere except the bilge.

CHAPTER IV

THE STOWAWAY

I attempted to search the bilge below the hold. The bilge had seawater, sewage, and stunk to high heaven. I quickly decided no one could stay down there for any length of time. Certainly not for several weeks, and immediately left the bilge.

"Had to take a crap?"

Startled I looked up and Pablo the friendly was standing there with that serious look on his face.

"No, sir!" I stood up straight.

"You looking for that stow away then? He won't be down here. He'll show himself eventually. Say, since you and I are alone..." His face became more serious.

Here it comes, I thought. Go left then right and go around him.

"I saw you the other night up at the bow. Not everyone is as friendly as me, boy. Mind yourself at night. You might fall overboard, and no one would ever know where you went."

I was getting more uneasy by the second "Okay, sir. I'll be careful. Can I go now?"

"Not so fast. I have another thing that's been bothering me. I've seen you before. That is, someone just like you. I'll remember one day. Best hope it's a nice memory boy. One more thing. The captain is strange, but you don't need to fear him. Most folks do. He's some kind of a witch, or warlock, or something. People get put in that cage of his, and next time anyone sees that man, he's no longer a man but a fish! Run along now."

Up the stairs, I went as fast as I could. I ran up to my quarters and sat in my hammock. *What was that all about? Where had he seen me before? He said he knows me. The captain is some sort of a witch? Is that why there is a cage in his room? Turned into a fish? Maybe that's what Goma had meant; they eat the fish! Where is the stowaway?*

It was getting dark, and I liked to watch the water turn a glowing blue from the wake of the ship. There was no one around. I saw a porpoise in front of the ship. I heard the short blow of air from his blowhole and watched him race the ship, the blue glow in the water outlining his movements. Then there was another and another. I leaned as far over the bow as I could and looked down to see what I could see.

There behind the bowsprit was a foot dangling. The sprit on the *Bella Donna* was a mermaid blowing a small horn. Below the sprit was a net. In the net was a man. I knew that man! He was asleep. His beard had grown, and he was thinner. It was Guiermo from the mountains. The man, some called Diablo.

I quickly withdrew. I sat there a moment thinking about what I should do. I finally decided that if I did nothing, I might dance the hempen jig along with him. Even though he was from my village, I really didn't know him well, but he had always been nice to me. On my way to find Goma, it came to me that I had to report him but maybe I could vouch for him as a good man. I found Goma on the upper deck with the navigator. They had a device looking up at a star.

"Mister Goma, sir. A word with you, if you please."

"My goodness, it must be serious. You have never addressed me this way. Then, by all means, speak. We are free people."

I relayed the story. He looked at the navigator. "Go fetch a couple of hands. We will retrieve this man. This stowaway!" Off the navigator went and returned only a short time later with three men carrying clubs. I was already regretting my decision.

"We have a stowaway as you know. Young Ramon here has found him. We will retrieve him. Try not to harm him until we know the captain's intentions. Ramon, you go fetch the captain. Use his main door, knock, and wait for him to open. Do not barge into his quarters."

This is getting worse by the second. I must wake up the captain. I approached the captain's door, rapped three times, and waited for an answer. The door swung open, and the captain was there looking down at me. A pistol in his left hand, which he quickly attempted to hide. I reported what was going on.

"Come along. We will wait on the main deck."

We went down and waited. A short time later the three men, the navigator, and Goma returned encircling the man as they approached the captain.

"What have you to say for yourself?" asked the captain.

"My name is Guiermo Angel Cruz. I have many trades. I'm also a marksman with a long gun." Guiermo didn't look up when he said this but seemed to be taking in his surroundings. His voice was calm.

"Why are you aboard my ship, and how did you get here?" asked the captain, in a more serious voice.

"I boarded her in San German. I blended in with your hands. When I had a chance, I slipped over the bow onto the sprit and fashioned a hammock there," Guiermo said without stuttering.

"So. You have been here all this time, and you did not starve to death. That could only mean you have been stealing our food!" The captain seemed to get a little taller. "Lock him in my cell!"

As quick as a blink. Guiermo elbowed Goma in the face, and Goma dropped to the floor out cold. He spun on the man to his left, placed an arm underneath the man's shoulder, spun around with a hip toss. The man landed with a thud. This happened so fast everyone else stood in disbelief. As they were realizing they were in a fight, Guiermo dropped another man with a palm strike to the side of his neck. He quickly spun to face the captain and was met with the butt of the captain's pistol to the forehead. Guiermo dropped to his knees. Blood was trailing into his eyes.

"Grab ahold of him and fetch the doc. Has everyone tended?" Said the captain. "Place him in the cell."

When Guiermo woke, he had a bandage wrapped around his head. He looked about and sat up slowly. His head was swimming. He looked about the room. The captain was sitting at his table. Looking at him but not saying anything. Minutes seemed like hours. Finally, Guiermo had enough. He sprung to his feet. He was intending to ask what was going to happen to him.

The only thing that came from his voice was gibberish, unrecognizable sounds in place of words. The room began to spin, and he fell to the floor.

Ramon brought the captain's meal and a bowl of soup for the prisoner. He had not been in the captain's quarters since Guiermo had been taken to the cell. He placed the items on the stool outside the door as he always did. He reached for the bell and the door opened.

The captain spoke, "You know this man? He comes from your village."

"Yes, sir. I know him, but he is not a friend of my family. He is always very nice to me. Some call him 'Diablo' because he gets angry and fights a lot. He is not a friend of the family, but he is not an enemy either."

"Diablo," repeated the captain. Not a question and not a statement.

"What will be done with him?"

"I haven't made up my mind yet. He is still out. He came to a little while ago. Jumped up and made some kind of noise and fell back to the floor again. I think maybe, I hit him too hard. Have you ever heard that this man killed anyone he fought with? I mean some men need killing. Most men are good down deep. But some men are born mean."

"I heard he fought off Dutch pirates once when he was younger. They tried to take over San German. My dad fought alongside him. My dad said he was a great fighter, and that's the real reason he is called 'El Diablo!'"

The captain thought for a moment, then said, "Well I haven't spoken with him. I will know more when he is better and fit to talk." He picked up the meals and turned to shut the door. "Go find the doc and send him here."

Three more days passed before Guiermo awoke again. He sat up slowly.

"Please! Do not stand up just yet. You are among my friends. We simply have not yet met," said Captain Gaza.

Guiermo looked at the captain, "Friends? I'm locked up in here!"

The captain stood and walked to the window overlooking aft, "We have mutual acquaintances. We have not discussed why you are here. Only how you got here."

"Believe me, Captain, if I knew you, I would remember. How long have I been out?"

The captain turned and faced him, "Almost two weeks. The doctor has been pouring a little soup at a time down your throat to keep you alive."

"Why? So I can dance the hempen jig?" Snapped Guiermo. "Two weeks?"

"Friends," replied the captain. "I will explain, but do not say anything to Ramon." The captain leaned forward, "I know his father. He does not know I know his father. When the time comes, I will enlighten him."

Guiermo stood slowly. "Maybe you should enlighten me first," he said in a low tone. "How do you mean you know his father? Maybe you do the right thing by telling me first." Guiermo was visibly angry. His face was that of a man who just discovered something bad and knew just how to handle the situation. Guiermo pointed a finger at the captain,

"I'll tell you about his father! His father was a good man. He disappeared one night, leaving a wife and two children to make do for themselves. Something he would not have ever done. Many times, I left money by the estufa. So, maybe you should tell me first. Just how do you know his father? Did you have a hand in his…leaving?"

"*Calma te*. Settle down! You remember you are my prisoner. We have a long time before reaching Puerto Rico, so I'll tell you a story of how I know his father." Captain Gaza turned and walked to his big table. He picked up a metal chalice and filled it with a clear liquid.

He walked over to Guiermo and handed him the chalice. Guiermo accepted the chalice and looked Gaza in the eyes.

Gaza returned the stare, "It is not poison. It is a drink I learned how to make in Puerto Rico. The Puerto Ricans cut sugar cane into small pieces and place the cane in a cask of water. Then they burry this cask for nearly a year. The results are what I was told, a type of rum called *canita*. It is very stout but good. I should warn you. Don't drink too much at one time. You will pass out! Save some for later, if you can."

Guiermo took a small sip. His eyebrows lifted a bit in approval. "This is very good. But I must tell you I am not given to strong drink. It makes me a little crazy and violent. I thank you for the drink. I will save it and sip it throughout the day." Guiermo took another swallow, this time more than a sip. He placed the chalice in the corner and sat down on his hammock. "I believe you were going to tell me a story."

"Ah, yes. I was going to tell you how I came to know our friend."

"You were? Now you're not?"

"If I let you out to sit at my table, will you behave yourself?"

Guiermo leaned forward. "I cannot make that promise."

CHAPTER V

SHANGHAIED

Captain Gaza pulled a chair close to the cell bars and sat down with his own chalice and sampled the *canita*. "That is quite good. The story starts in your own port of San German."

The sun was going down. Reynaldo Molina and his five-year-old son Ramon were sitting beneath a Guanacaste tree outside their house. The view overlooked the mountain and sea just outside San German. They watched as a ship neared the harbor below. They couldn't see the entire harbor but knew the ship was going there.

"That's a brigantine," Reynaldo explained to Ramon. It has two masts, and they are able to attach other sails called gaffs to the mast in front. That mast is called the foremast. They can attach more gaff sails to the aft of the mainmast too."

Ramon looked up at his father, "What is a mast, Poppy?" Ramon was enjoying the time he was spending with his father.

Reynaldo laughed, "The masts are the two tree-like things, sticking up in the air."

Just then Ramon's mother, Lupe, came to the front door. "Okay, gentlemen, it's time to eat."

As they ate their meal Reynaldo said to Lupe, "I'm going into town tonight. Some of the men are meeting, and I want to look at that ship. We don't need another incident with pirates."

Lupe looked at Reynaldo, "Just please be careful, and don't be too late."

After the meal Reynaldo gave Ramon a hug and a kiss on the forehead, "You go to sleep now. I'll see you in the morning."

Reynaldo made his rounds and kissed Rena, his baby girl, and then Lupe. "I love my little family. Don't wait up." Reynaldo took his wife's chin between his thumb and forefinger, kissed her lips, and then her forehead. He took two steps and turned back around, "I don't know what's wrong with me, I just feel like staying home."

Lupe smiled at him, "Go. The town meeting is important. Don't drink too much afterward." That was Lupe's way of saying it's ok to have a drink but do not get drunk.

Reynaldo walked out the door and down the trail towards the town. When he reached the harbor, there was a lamp lighted at the end of the peer. There were crates and bundles stacked on the peer awaiting shipment. Reynaldo walked past these and onto the lamp. He stood in the glow of the lamp and admired the scene. He saw the ship. She had lamps that were lit in the fortress and scattered about the upper deck. The lamps cast light all about. The lights gave her a mystical but beautiful appearance. *Wow. That's a beautiful ship!* He thought. Reynaldo turned to continue on his way to the meeting. As he turned, something hit his head and a bright light flashed before his eyes.

There was a subtle creaking noise in his ears. Faint voices seem to come and go. His bed swayed gently back and forth. *The voices again. I wish they would leave. My god, why does my head hurt?* "Lupe!" He cried out. The voices stopped. *Gracias A Dios! Make the pain go away Jesus. Por favor!*

"You should not have hit him so hard! What do you think Goma? Will he survive?" asked Captain Soto.

First Mate Gaza replied, "Yes, Captain. He called out to someone a little while ago. 'Lupe,' he said."

Lorenzo, one of the hands spoke, "My grandmother, she had a dog one time who had a kick to the head by a horse. The dog was knocked out like this man. That dog cried out for two or three days. That dog, he did not survive."

Captain Soto looked at Lorenzo, "Go find something to do."

Lorenzo's feelings seemed hurt, "Okay, I go. I did not mean to hit so hard. Maybe he has a soft head or something! I don't know!"

First Mate Gaza stepped towards Lorenzo, "Go!" he said. Lorenzo turned and walked away sulking and mumbling.

Reynaldo felt his legs come to life. They were numb and tingling. His head still hurt, and he was hungry.

"I think he is coming around captain. I saw his foot move and he made a grimace on his face," said Dias Gaza.

The captain stood from behind his big table, "Maybe you should tell the cook to bring him something to eat. Something, not soup, but easy on the stomach."

Gaza promptly left the cell and closed the door behind him. It was the clanging shut of the door that brought Reynaldo to open his eyes. He lay there looking around with his eyes only. He could smell the sea. He heard noises of creaking timbers, like when the wind blows in the forest. *But I am not in the forest*, he thought. He realized he was in a hammock.

His eyes began to clear and for the first time, he knew where he was. "I'm on a ship," he shouted. What am I doing on a ship?" His voice caused a lightning bolt of pain to shoot through his head. He attempted to get out of the hammock and fell onto the floor. He heard footsteps approaching. He managed to sit up and lean his back against the wall. Reynaldo looked up at the man in front of him. Average in height and build. He wore a white shirt, black britches, and high boots oiled to a bright black shine. He wore a red sash on his waist. His hair was cut close to the scalp. His face is clean-shaven. The man stood there looking down at him.

"What shall I do with you?" the man asked.

"You brought me here. You tell me! What shall you do with me?" The two men looked at each other. It was clear the two had no liking for one another. "Can you at least tell me where we are and how long I have been out?"

"We are near Venezuela bearing south. You have been on this ship for nearly two weeks. I wasn't sure you were going to survive," replied the man. "Let me properly introduce myself. I am Javier Guadalupe Soto, captain of the *Bella Donna*."

Reynaldo managed for the first time to stand, still leaning on the wall. He proudly lifted his head and said, "I am Reynaldo Molina. Father of Ramon and Rena Molina. Faithfull husband of Lupe Angelina Molina." He calmly stared at Soto. "I have only one thing left to say, Capitan Soto! 'Vengeance is mine saith the Lord.' But I will not wait on my Lord! I will have my vengeance!"

"You may well indeed. I could not blame you. However, you are behind bars, are you not?"

Reynaldo smiled, "Well, that is a minor detail. Sooner or later that door will open."

Captain Soto rubbed his chin as if in thought. "Do you think you could hold off your vengeance until we have had a good meal and a glass of rum?"

"I am hungry and very thirsty."

The two men sat at the big table, ate, and talked well into the night. Captain Soto explained to him that it was not his command to shanghai anyone. The man responsible was told to recruit men. The man who is called Lorenzo mistook the command to mean, any way possible.

They talked of years past and possibilities of the future. They found each other's company interesting. Reynaldo told Captain Soto of the battle for San German against Dutch pirates determined to take over the small port.

Captain Soto poured another goblet of Canita. "I am sorry you were taken from your family. I will return you as soon as I possibly can. First, I must complete a task given to me by a dear friend. We must sail to Colombia to make a delivery and pick up a small load to deliver on the African coast. That will take months."

"Months? My family has no way of knowing what has happened to me. They will think me dead or simply abandoned my family."

"I will do what I can. In the meantime, stay close. I will treat you as my first mate."

The captain and Reynaldo became close friends over several months. Reynaldo proved to be a fast learner. The crew liked him. He spent a lot of time with them listening to their stories. He took interest in each sailor. He enjoyed their singing at night and the games they played.

He learned how to navigate by the stars at night. He could read and write. He assisted the captain in logging each daily event. He tried to stay busy so the time would pass, and he would be back home.

CHAPTER VI

COLOMBIA

The *Bella Donna* sailed into Colombia waters. The wind was favorable, and the skies were clear. Simón Bolivar was waiting for the *Bella Donna*. He heard the ship was in the waters. Simón Bolivar was born in Venezuela and gained a reputation and nickname, the Liberator.

Captain Soto and Reynaldo had been spending a lot of time together talking theology and battle strategy. Reynaldo knew very little about sea battle but had proven himself many times in battle on land.

"Sails to the south!" came a yell from the watch. "Bearing north!"

Captain Soto and Reynaldo jump to their feet. They ran out onto the upper deck. The captain produced a field glass, "She travels alone?" Captain Soto carefully, but as quickly as possible, scanned all the way around looking for other ships, for a trap. "That is Simón Bolivar's ship." He made the statement as if it were a thought made out loud.

"Make ready for battle, First Mate Gaza!"

"Hoay!" shouted First Mate Gaza. "Make ready for battle!"

Men began to scuttle about the deck, weapons in hand. Every man had his eye patch on his forehead ready to pull down if needed. The cannon hatches were opened. The cannons are primed and ready for action. Reynaldo asked, "Have you a musket, Captain? I am a decent aim. I've not had much experience with a saber." He was pointed in the direction to arm himself. Reynaldo chose a musket, a short sword, and two pistols.

All settled down. The only noise was the creak of the timbers, the ocean, and the wind in the sails. As Bolivar's ship neared a white flag unfurled from the main. "Steady men," said Captain Soto. "It could be a ploy. Maintain your weapons! Do nothing until I say!"

A longboat was lowered with just three men in the boat. The longboat came to the *Bella Donna*. There were two older men and a younger man. The younger wore the captain's uniform. Reynaldo looked at Captain Soto, "He can only be in his early twenties."

Captain Soto responded, "Yes! He is young and very savvy. Notice his ship is a broadside of us and with twice the guns."

"He will meet with us, size us up, and decide to leave us or sink us." He turned and faced Reynaldo and Gaza, "Sit in on the palaver with us. We are united as a crew, and we are diverse. We are neither French, Spaniard, Portuguese, nor Dutch, though we have men who are. Bolivar hates Spain." He followed up with, "It seems almost all countries do these days."

The event with Bolivar was short. He was on his way to meet with Jose de San Martin, an Argentine revolutionary. They were planning to liberate Peru from Spain's control. They met briefly. Bolivar decided the *Bella Donna* was in the waters of Colombia with good intentions.

"I wish you were free to join us. We could use another ship in the liberation of Peru."

"Maybe we can assist you elsewhere at another time," replied Captain Soto, being very diplomatic.

"Perhaps."

The two captains departed.

It wasn't until the *Bella Donna* encountered a Dutch warship that Reynaldo proved himself as a fighter and a just man. Captain Soto was seriously injured in battle. Reynaldo fought in the mingle of men punching, slashing, and shooting. He was a driven man when it came to battle. The drive in him was the desire to see his family once again. When the battle was over there were only four men left standing, and the Dutch ship was listing and taken on water. She was sinking fast.

The ship's doctor came from the captain's quarters. He approached First Mate Gaza and Reynaldo. In a low, shaking voice he whispered, "The Captain is dead."

Reynaldo stood over one of the enemies with his right foot on the man's neck. Reynaldo was a fierce sight. There was hardly an inch of his body that wasn't covered in blood. The doctor gave Reynaldo a piece of paper. He read it and gave the paper to First Mate Gaza.

"Hoay!" Shouted Gaza. Captain Soto is dead! With his hand he has pinned his wishes and last command. This will be placed on the door of the captain's quarters for all to read. Captain Soto has named me the captain of the *Bella Donna* and Reynaldo the First Mate."

Reynaldo spoke up, "Hoay. There will be a manuscript beside the letter. Make your mark that you have read it. We will hear any contest you may have."

"What about these men?" Someone yelled.

Reynaldo wiped the blood from his face. "Bring all that remains alive, forward."

The three other Dutchmen were shoved forward on the main deck. Reynaldo stood on the edge of the upper deck, his foot still on the Dutch sailor's neck. Gripping both hands on the railing and looking down on the three men.

"Make them dance the hempen jig," came a voice. Several men shouted in agreement.

"Walk the plank!" came another voice.

Reynaldo lifted his hands in a gesture to silence the men. "These men have attacked us. We did nothing to provoke an attack. They will be judged here and now. The sentence will be served as quick. What say ye men?" The crew became quiet. "We are men of honor and just men, and they will be justly treated!"

The crew stood silent as Reynaldo held their attention. He stood there covered in blood from the lives he had taken and his voice seemed to thunder such as they had not heard before. "What say ye men of war?"

He reached down and jerked the Dutch sailor onto his feet. "What have you to say for yourself?"

"I only followed orders," said the man.

Reynaldo asked each man. The following two repeated the first man. The fourth man stiffened his shoulders. "We saw a beautiful ship full of ugly, mangy, no good, scum, and we thought to kill you all and take your ship."

Reynaldo let the count of three go by. He then, without a word, sliced the throat of the Dutch sailor standing just in front of him. "Judgement has been passed! Kill them and throw them to Davy Jones's locker!"

The crew accepted the new order of leadership without question. The *Bella Donna* gave Captain Soto a burial at sea.

Reynaldo became known as Reynaldo the Judge. After a battle, any survivors were offered a chance to give their witness and testimony before receiving a quick and decisive conviction. Join the crew or die depending on the testimony given.

"As time went by Reynaldo the Judge became known as a fierce but just man. He became my best friend. I consider him to be my brother and therefore his son to be my family.

Guiermo stood and walked to the windows, "So, you knew Reynaldo well?"

Captain Gaza remained sitting. "Yes. We were very close. The man was well respected by many."

"What about Ramon? Does he know about his father?" asked Guiermo.

Captain Gaza cleared his throat, "I have not spoken to him about his father. I have heard he has been asking questions of some of the men. No one is saying anything to him about Reynaldo 'The Judge' Molina.

"So, where is he now?"

"We were overtaken by a Turkish ship. There was a long battle. Reynaldo was injured and fell into the water. A longboat from the Turkish ship plucked him from the water. I assumed he was dead. As far as I knew, I was the only one still alive. Then last year we liberated a slave ship bound for Puerto Rico and Port Royale. They had been taken just off the Barbary Coast. One of the slaves knew Reynaldo from a

Turkish prison. He said the Turks use him for translating and keeping up with documents."

Guiermo took a step towards Captain Gaza, "If it would please you, sir, I would be honored to go with you."

Captain Gaza smiled, "Do you forget so soon that you are a stow-away? That is a matter that must be dealt with. The men would not understand if I just let you walk around the ship without any explanation."

"Sir! I have fought many battles alongside Reynaldo Molina. I would rather die fighting for his freedom than dance the hemp en jig."

"You are a fighter. You took out a couple of my men with hardly an effort." Captain Gaza looked at Guiermo for a long second, "I tell you what. You will be judged, and your sentence will be to fight one of my men. A man of my choosing. Not to the death just to whoever stops fighting or is unable to fight further."

Proudly Guiermo stuck out his hand. Then quickly withdrew it, "What happens if I lose? I still dance the hempen jig?"

Captain Gaza shook his head, "No, no, either way, you will be a member and most respected among the crew. We will all sail to the Barbary Coast and the prison that holds Reynaldo."

"Ramon," shouted Captain Gaza.

I jumped to my feet. I entered the captain's quarters. I saw Guiermo and Captain Gaza standing in the center of the room. "Captain?"

"Ramon, go fetch First Mate Sanchez and Vincent. When you have found both, then the three of you report back here."

I looked at Guiermo. He gave a smile and a nod as if to say I'll be alright. "Yes, Captain! Right away." I ran from the room and hustled down to the main deck. The first person I ran into was Snake. "Sir, have you seen First Mate Sanchez?"

"Yesss," he said, leaning on a mop handle.

I waited for a second, "Well?"

"Of course, I have ssseen him. I don't know where he isss right now."

"Dios mio!" I said and promptly continued my search. I found First Mate Sanchez in the hold. I reported what the captain had said, and he knew exactly where to find Vincent.

"Vincent will be in his hammock. He takes a siesta this time of day," said Sanchez.

We found Vincent sound asleep. I took a step towards him, and Sanchez grabbed my arm. "Stay right here. If you startle him, he will hurt you before he even wakes." First Mate Sanchez grabbed a broom, tapped on the hammock, and said softly, "Vincent! Vincent?"

Vincent sprung to his feet, "What in the bloody hell?" He stood there braced for who knows what. I could see the recognition come into his eyes.

"Young Ramon, First Mate. Please excuse me, sir." Vincent said in his thick accent.

I relayed the message from the captain, "Did I do something to vex the captain?" he asked.

We made our way to the captain's quarter and reported. "The men, as you ordered sir," I snapped.

The captain stood up. Guiermo stayed seated, with an amused look on his face.

"This man is Guiermo. As you know he is a stowaway. However, the two of us have a mutual, show we say, desire for a certain adventure. I find Guiermo will be a great asset to this adventure. However, he is a stowaway."

The men were looking at each other in confusion. Sanchez spoke, "Sir, it is not my place to ask, but why is this man not locked up? You saw what he is capable of."

The captain placed his chalice on the table and looked squarely at First Mate Sanchez. "You're correct Sanchez! It is not your place to ask." All were quiet for a minute. "Now if you don't mind, I will continue. There has to be a reckoning. What is going to happen is this. There will be a match, a fight. This fight will be on the main deck. Sanchez will make the announcement. Guiermo and Vincent …

"Capitan! I have no cause to fight this man. If you want to kill him, kill him," exclaimed Vincent.

"I do not want you to kill him. I believe you are the man most capable of lasting long enough to appease the crew. You both will fight until one of you can fight no more. However, neither of you will kill the other! Are we clear on that matter?"

Vincent was uneasy, "Captain I have never fought without a reason."

The captain walked over to Vincent and stood toe to toe. He looked up into the face of the big black man. "This is the only way the crew will be satisfied without killing the man. He pointed his finger at Guiermo," This is a man who will help us win many battles to come. The captain raised his voice. He will fight or dance the hempen jig."

Guiermo stood, "I can come over and slap you if you want me to. That will give you a reason to fight! After all, you will be saving my life. I'm going to fight like a demon monkey to please the crew! It's a lot better than Davy Jones's locker!"

Vincent gave Guiermo a look over, "Very well, Captain, it shall be."

The men left the quarters. I was on his way out. The captain spoke, "Ramon! Stay. We need to talk."

I walked back to the captain. "Please sit down," the captain said. There is something we need to discuss man to man."

"Yes, Captain," I took a seat."

"Would you care for some *canita*?"

"No, sir, Captain," *What did I do wrong?* Suddenly I blurted out, "I promise, sir, I had no idea Guiermo was on the ship."

"No. I'm sure you did not. I wish to speak to you of your father."

I felt a sick feeling coming up in my throat, like when you eat something disagreeable to your stomach. "Sir?"

"I knew your father very well. I was the first mate on this very ship the evening Reynaldo Molina was shanghaied."

"He was shanghaied, sir?" not believing my ears. "Did you…"

"No! No, he wasn't supposed to be shanghaied! I had nothing to do with it. That changes nothing."

I sat there without interrupting as the captain told the story of my father. My head was lite. At times I wanted to cry, and at times I was elated.

My father is alive!

Captain Gaza continued, "In that battle with the Turkish ship, he was wounded and fell overboard. He was taken captive by the Turks and just before we came to San German, I heard the news he is alive and well, on the Barbary Coast."

I jumped to my feet, "My father is alive? Wait! If he is alive, why did he not return home? He has been gone…"

"For ten years. Yes, I know. Your father has been in a Turkish prison on the Barbary Coast. He was not free to leave."

I was now pacing around in the room. My head was swimming. I could not form a complete thought. I suddenly felt sick and weak. I sat down and stared out the window for what seemed to be an eternity.

The captain placed a hand on my shoulder, "The reason for coming to San German was not just to replenish. I was planning on coming to your home and revealing the information to Reynaldo's family. Also, to advise your family that we were going to retrieve him and bring him home."

I looked at the captain, "Is that where we are going now?"

The captain smiled, "Yes. First, we will stop in Puerto Rico. That is if all is well. Simón Bolivar will be on the Island of Vieques.

It is 1816, Ramon. In 1803, Denmark abolished the slave trade and Britain in 1807. There are others like us who don't approve of the slave trade. That is why we seek out ships carrying slaves. Dutch, French, it does not matter.

We seek them out and free those we can. The Caribbean is full of islands from people who were once slaves. They are called *Caribes*. Simón Bolivar and all his ships will be at Vieques. We will meet with him. After we liberate Puerto Rico from Spain. We will leave from there and sail to Tripoli in North Africa."

"All these men would do this for my father?" I asked.

Captain Gaza leaned towards me. "Yes! Your father would do the same for them without a second thought. He is a just man and a fierce fighter! If you are in the wrong, you will pay. Your father is also known as 'The Judge.' If he finds you guilty, he is quickly the executioner."

There was suddenly a commotion on the main deck. I jumped to my feet. The captain grabbed me by my shoulder. "Wait! Listen, and then we will look."

"*Hoay*! Dutch merchant to the stern," came a yell from the lookout.

Captain Gaza snatched up his spyglass and focused on the ship. "Dutch alright! She is by herself. That's no merchant ship. Too many guns. Come on!" We went out onto the fortress deck. First Mate Sanchez was waiting.

"Make ready for battle First Mate Sanchez!" ordered the captain. "Slow but steady. Let her catch up!"

First Mate Sanchez relayed the order. Men were running around on the deck and below deck. I noticed they all wore an eye patch on their forehead. I asked Guiermo about the patches.

Guiermo handed me a patch, "The patch will keep one eye dark so if you go in a room from outside, you lift the patch and the eye will be ready to see in the darkened room. Otherwise, you will be blind for a moment while your eyes adjust. A moment that could end your life."

Men were rolling out cannons. Nine-inch cannons and packing them with the shot. Some were loaded with two balls that had a chain attached to each ball. I had never seen such a thing. On top of the fortress, Guiermo and six other marksmen were lying down with long guns. I heard the doors on the hatches open and looked down the side of the ship. Cannons began to appear from the portholes. Twelve cannons below deck. These were larger than the eight cannons on the main deck.

I heard thunder and there was suddenly a huge splash directly behind the ship, too close for comfort.

"Ramon," snapped the captain. He handed me a pistol, "Go to my quarters. Stay away from the windows! There are several more pistols in the trunk next to the table. Beneath the table is another. Shoot anyone that comes through that door. Everyone knows not to go through that door! Anyone who does will be an enemy!"

I ran to the captain's quarters and located the pistols. I checked each one. An unloaded gun is nothing more than a club. I sat there a while. I heard First Mate Sanchez yell out an order, "Raise the gaffs! Run out the ores!" I could hear the creaking of timbers as the gaff sails grabbed the wind. I could sense the ship picking up speed. I heard the thunder again and the splash was further away from the *Bella Donna*. I heard another shout from First Mate Sanchez, "Port side, all reverse!" *Reverse!* I thought. Suddenly the ship violently tilted to the port side and things began falling from the shelves. The *Bella Donna* suddenly righted herself, and all hell broke loose from the cannons above and below deck.

Even though I was told not to go near the windows, I ran to one corner and knelt to peek at what was going on. The other ship was a lot closer than I thought she would be. The *Bella Donna* was now broadside to the Dutch ship. The chained double cannonballs had done their work.

The idea of the two cannonballs chained together, the chain between the two balls would slice through timbers and men with horrendous damage. As I watched, the foremast of the Dutch warship was falling, cut into by the chains. The sails were tattered. The Dutch ship was now in no shape to give chase. I could tell the *Bella Donna* was in a pattern to circle around the now crippled Dutch ship.

First Mate Sanchez shouted again, "Fire!"

The cannons as one fired again some missed most did not. There was smoke coming from the other ship now.

"Fire at will," commanded First Mate Sanchez.

There was a steady staccato of explosions coming from the *Bella Donna* as the cannons cleared their throat.

If we continue this course, we will be the broad side of that ship, and she has bigger and more guns! As if the captain read my thoughts the *Bella Donna* was heading almost straight for the Dutch warship. The cannons were firing less frequently now that we were no longer broadside. Now the marksmen began to fire independently as targets presented themselves.

I started to hear hard thuds against the outside walls. Suddenly the window on the opposite side exploded inward. The crew of the Dutch ship were firing now.

They were in every way, literally fighting for their lives. Smaller deck cannons were firing. These were filled with anything that could be placed down the barrel.

I forced myself to peek out the window again. We were now alongside the Dutch ship. The *Bella Donna* had come alongside the disabled ship from her bow therefore drawing very little cannon fire. Men from both ships were throwing grappling hooks trying to pull the ships together to fight man to man.

There was yelling and cursing. The clanging of swords and pistol shots. I saw a man fall into the water and realized there were many men floating. Sharks had caught the scent of the blood in the water, and they were in a frenzy. The sight of sharks seemed to block out everything else.

I recognized one of the men in the water. It was the man the crew called Snake. I recognized his face. He wasn't dead. He must have been knocked overboard or perhaps he had fallen. Just as I recognized him, he violently was pulled under in a pool of red water and a giant gray tail fin.

I barely registered what I had just seen when the door suddenly burst open. A man in a red and white uniform stopped just inside the door.

The man had no eye patch to guard his vision. The man was covered in blood. In his right hand was a pistol. In the other was a saber. He was straining to see in the darkroom.

I trained my pistol on the man's chest. His eyes had not adjusted to the darkroom. He stood there not moving for what seemed like an eternity. Suddenly the man saw me and charged.

I didn't seem to think about killing the man. Suddenly, the pistol in my hand jumped and the man was knocked backward, landed on his back, and didn't move.

I dropped that pistol and grabbed the one from under the table, and none too soon. Another man entered the room scanning the dim room. I fired again. That man dropped just inside the door. I dropped that pistol and ran for the chest. *Is everyone dead?* I asked myself. I grabbed another pistol and heard heavy steps enter the room I spun and was about to fire the pistol.

"Ramon, it's me your Captain!"

I snapped out of it and a surge of emotions swept over me.

The captain was standing there looking at me seemingly astonished, "Did you...," asked the captain motioning at the two men.

"Yes, sir," I said feeling that maybe I had done something horrible.

"Are you okay? Are you hurt?" The captain asked as he walked slowly towards me. "Do you still have a pistol? Please lay the pistol on the table, Ramon." His concern was valid as I realized, I still had the pistol from the chest pointed right at him. His question, "Do you still have a pistol?" made me realize I did indeed still have one and brought me back to my senses.

The *Bella Donna* was now free from the Dutch ship. The captain walked over to me. He placed his hand on my shoulder and gently removed the pistol. "Help me with this sailor. He is still alive."

This was the second man that had entered the room. The pistol from beneath the table was a smaller pistol. The man was not dead but wounded and though unconscious, was still alive. I helped the captain place the man in the cell.

We crossed back over to the now, listing Dutch ship. I noticed everyone had a patch over one eye. First Mate Sanchez handed a patch to me. "This is so when we enter a dark area of the ship you will be able to see from that eye when you lift the patch."

"Thanks!" I didn't tell him I already had one.

First Mate Sanchez, with a sword in hand, ordered the men to search the ship for fresh food, water, and rum—anything that can be useful to the crew. He looked at me, "Come with me, Ramon." We went to the captain's quarters. The door was not even locked. The Dutch captain was seated in his chair at a table. He was slumped over with a pistol lying on the floor next to him. I lifted the patch and sure enough, I could see better.

"He couldn't stand the shame of losing his ship I guess," I said.

First Mate Sanchez nodded in agreement, "Look around for maps, logbooks—anything of that sort. Valuable information is sometimes kept in them."

After scouring the room and finding the logbook and schedule, we went to join the other men to search the hold. The ship was listing on the port side now to the point we could hardly walk upright.

As we entered the hold, we detected the foul odor of human waste. Suddenly one of the men shouted, "First Mate Sanchez! We have men here sir. Chained men!"

"Damn the Dutch! This is no merchant ship. They are slavers!"

I had never seen such a thing. Men, women, children. Black, white, and Spanish, all chained up like animals.

Vincent stepped up, "Everyone grabs something, hammers—anything to free these people. We don't have much time."

Just then a chained black man rattled something off I couldn't understand. I looked to where he was pointing and saw a dead man lying over a barrel. In his hand were keys. I quickly retrieved the keys and tossed them to Vincent who wasted no time in freeing the people. They were all excited now. A mother ran to her child who couldn't have been more than eight years of age. There were three women one younger than me. They were naked, facing the wall with their hands fastened to it with a short chain. It took no explanation as to why! Vincent quickly released them. I grabbed three shirts and gave one to each. The tallest woman looked at me and said, "May I have your pistol too?" She took my pistol before I could protest, placed it against her head, and pulled the trigger.

I was frozen. I slowly picked up my pistol and looked at Vincent. He had a sad look on his face. Not the smiling one I was used to. He broke the silence.

Vincent ordered, "Everyone top side now she won't stay upright very much longer! Move! Move! Move!"

We wasted no time getting everyone aboard the *Bella Donna*. "They were taking us to Puerto Rico to sell us," said a white man.

Captain Gaza replied, "We too are going to Puerto Rico. To an island called Vieques. We are to meet up with an ally who has 8 ships and 400 men. We aim to liberate Puerto Rico from Spain which is occupying her. Once there, any man who feels strong enough can join us in the fight."

As if on command the Dutch ship gave a loud groan and rolled onto its port side. Everyone made it out of the slave ship just in time. As we were sailing away, I looked back to see her aft sink beneath the waves. It was a spooky kind of feeling. *That could have been us on any day.*

CHAPTER VII

PUERTO RICO

Two days later we landed at Vieques. It was not a large island. There, anchored off her south beach were the eight ships we were hoping to find.

"Lower a longboat," shouted First Mate Sanchez. "Lower a Jacob's ladder." Immediately the men were busy as ordered. The longboat was let down, and the Jacob's ladder was dropped over the side. The captain was going to solidify the joining of our crew with Simón Bolivar.

The skies were dark. The clouds were moving from the east by southeast at an unbelievable speed. The waves seemed to be higher and unsettled. The men were busying themselves battening down hatches and stowing anything lose in the ship, above and below deck. The slaves rescued from the Dutch ship had made their own camp. Most of the men had joined Bolivar's crew of 400 men.

Captain Bolivar and eight captains sat around a fire on the lee side of a dune. The fire was whipping around almost alive. Captain Bolivar looked at the skies for a moment then turned his attention to the other eight captains, "This is a sizeable force. No doubt the Spanish know we are here. Before this storm hits, we will sail due north for one day. Anchor for one day and return in the darkness of the second night. We should arrive off of the north coast just outside the harbor. The harbor is protected by El Morro. A very stout fortress. If we spread thin from El Moro east and bombard at daybreak it will draw attention. The *Bella*

Donna will make landfall east of El Morro and march by land towards El Morro. We will lay siege from both sides, north and south."

Captain Garza looked around at the skies, "Captain Bolivar, I think the plan is sound. I also think there is a hurricane approaching. If we sail north as planned, we might be out of its reach before it gets here."

Captain Bolivar shook his head in agreement. "Let's get everyone on deck and sail due north." The crews wasted no time, and the nine ships were sailing due north. The hurricane was moving west by northwest. I was in the captain's quarters seated across from the captain. He was filling me in on the history of Puerto Rico as best he could. "A Dutch expedition under the command of Hendricks attacked the island but, even after taking over San Juan for two months, was unable to capture it from Spain. I think this is a losing campaign I have gotten us into."

It was clear Captain Garza was uneasy about the battle about to take place. "Captain. Why don't we just leave?"

"We can't do that, Ramon. We gave… I gave my word. We will support Bolivar in his endeavor to free Puerto Rico from the clutches of Spain. A man is only as good as his word."

Just then First Mate Goma entered the quarters. "Sir, there is a matter of the stowaway. The crew is starting to grumble that he was never dealt with properly."

Captain Gaza stood and leaned forward with both fists on the table, "Even after his fighting and showing how ruthless he can be? My god, I think he killed half the Dutchmen on that ship!"

The captain seemed to relax a bit and walked over to the windows. "Very well. Send the two men here. We have a long day just sitting here. A little entertainment might do them some good."

A few minutes later and Vincent and Guiermo were standing in front of the captain, "You know, men. There is this matter still on the table about the acceptance of Guiermo as a crew member."

"Aw, captain," said Vincent. "I thought all that mess was over. He done fought tooth and nail. He drew blood and risked his own life for this ship."

"Or maybe I didn't have a choice. What was I to do, hide?"

"First Mate Goma is already gathering the men on the main deck. Remember! Do not kill one another. Fight a good fight but do not maim or kill each other. You both understand?" The captain turned his head sideways. "They have gathered already. Can you hear them?"

"After this is over and I'm still game, can I punch a few of them," Guiermo asked with a smile.

"That would make the entire fight pointless. The idea is to gain their friendship, not their hatred," said Captain Gaza.

We opened the door and there was an immediate uproar. "Spank him good, Vincent," said someone. The entire ship was yelling and cheering. I looked over at another ship, and the crew were lining the decks trying to see what was happening on board the *Bella Donna*. First Mate Goma gave a short speech about justice and forgiveness and was interrupted by the shouting of the men to "get on with it."

Both men were bare-chested and sweating. Vincent began to circle Guiermo.

Guiermo lightly through a punch to gauge the reaction of the big man. Vincent didn't flinch. "Humph," said Guiermo.

As quick as lightning Vincent struck Guiermo square on the chin. Guiermo staggered backward and was shoved back into the circle. Vincent smiled his big smile, "That wake you up, stowaway?"

The crew cheered. Guiermo ran a short three steps leaped into the air and kicked Vincent in the chest, landed on both feet, and squared off to throw another punch. Vincent was shoved into the crowd. The crowd shoved him back into the circle.

Now the crew was really excited. Never had they seen anyone stand up in a fight after Vincent threw the first punch. Not only did Guiermo continue standing but knocked the big man into the crowd. Vincent came roaring back in with the shove from the crew. Guiermo sidestepped and shot a right to the left side of Vincent's head just behind the ear. Vincent's knees buckled, and he dropped down on all fours. Guiermo stood wide-legged, fists clenched, and his right fist cocked back as far as he could, for a blow to the face if Vincent looked up.

The blow would end the fight. Vincent did look up and immediately Guiermo shot the fist down towards Vincent's jaw. Mid swing Vincent looked back down but it was too late. Guiermo could not stop the punch. The target had presented itself and the blow was en route. The blow landed on the back of Vincent's head. Vincent sprawled out on the deck.

The crowd was silent. Everyone's eyes switched from Vincent, who some saw as invincible, to Guiermo the new wonder on the *Bella Donna*.

Guiermo backed up two steps. *This could be bad. That looked to be an intentional dirty blow! Guiermo was thinking.*

Suddenly the big black man sprung to his feet standing tall. Guiermo's eyes grew wide.

"So, man. That's how you fight? Like a woman? You hit in the back of the head? This is not war, my friend." Vincent stepped forward on bent knees and swung an uppercut straightening and twisting his hip as the uppercut caught underneath Guiermo's chin. The full force of his legs and arms was at the meeting point with Guiermo's chin. Into the air Guiermo went and landed flat on his back, sprawled out on the deck.

The crew was ecstatic. I stood there half afraid Guiermo was dead. The punch was hard and sounded dull and solid. I walked over to Guiermo, and I could see he was breathing.

"He will be okay, Ramon. He's just sleeping. That's a man who can fight on my side anytime." said a man. The rest of the crew agreed.

Vincent walked over to me and looked down into my eyes, "I had to end this quickly. I couldn't take much more from that man. I had to end it quickly." The crowd burst out again, "Vincent! Vincent! Vincent!"

Four of the men picked Guiermo up and carried him down below deck. I looked at the captain, "It's okay! They are going to take care of him if he needs the care. They will let him sleep it off. It's their way of showing approval."

I looked at Vincent. "Are you okay?"

He smiled, "A little hungry but okay!"

The rest of the day went smoothly. The sea was unusually calm. One of the crew members caught a huge gray fish. I thought it was a shark, but the man said it was something called a lemon fish or something like that. The fish was cleaned and prepared for supper, and it fed the entire crew. We were getting ready to return to Puerto Rico to fight against the Spanish fortress, El Moro. There was no doubt that this could be the last meal some of these brave men would have and everyone knew it. As we set sail just after sunset everyone was preparing for battle.

The night grew long. In the far distance I could see lightning. At times it looked like the bars of a jail cell, like the cell in the captain's quarters. The lighting covered the horizon.

The captain joined me on the fortress deck, "It's beautiful is it not?"

"Yes, sir. I've never seen anything like that." I hesitated. "Captain? Will we ever get to the Barbary Coast? Will I ever see my father?"

Captain Gaza looked at me, "Hell itself will not keep us from retrieving your father! As soon as this business is done, we will set off for the Barbary coast, and we will not stop except for food and water. If I can help it there will be no further delays."

I smiled, "I think I will turn in now. Tomorrow is not a sure thing! I mean I hope we all survive." I turned and walked away. I could feel the captain's eyes on my back as I left. I climbed in my hammock and lay there listening to the water whispering to the ship as it passed the hull. Once I heard a pod of porpoise blowing as they breached the surface seeming to race the ship in their playful ways.

I awoke startled by a ruckus of the crew scampering about the deck. I hardly helped in the kitchen these days except to bring the captain his food. I jumped up and peered outside. It was breaking day, and I could see an island due south of us. One thing that stood out was a huge fortress. *Puerto Rico, El Morro!* The captain was already on the deck with his long "spy glass." First Mate Goma stood by his side. Guiermo was there also with a bandage around his head and chin. I walked over to Guiermo, "You should not have hit him in the back of the head!" Guiermo chuckled in a muffled sound. His chin was bound up tight. He attempted to say something, but I couldn't understand him.

"He said, he didn't intend to, but I turned my head in mid swing. He also said he learned his lesson." Vincent said as he walked up behind me.

Smoke bellowed from El Moro. It was a full two seconds before we heard the report. Of course, we were well out of range.

"Approximately two miles out. That was a warning shot. Turn the ship east," said Captain Gaza.

First Mate Goma repeated the command, and we started heading east. I ran aft where I could see. The other eight ships were positioned for a broadside. They were closer to El Morro than we were because they were basically the distraction from the *Bella Donna*. All eight ships fired their cannons one after another giving the first ship to fire plenty of time to assess and reload.

I couldn't see if there was damage to the fortress, but I had my doubts after seeing that stone fortress. We were nearly out of sight when the sails were lowered, and the crew broke out the ores. No one was saying a word. We were a hundred men strong with crewmen from the other eight ships bearing long guns, pistols, and swords.

The captain and just enough men stayed on the *Bella Donna* and went back out, to ensure the ship would still be there when we returned.

"Stay close to me and Guiermo," commanded Vincent. Since the fight those two were inseparable.

We quickly left the white sand beach for the forest. It was mostly, low thick green, leafy brush with the canopy covered with palm trees. It wasn't but a few feet, and we came upon a well-traveled oxcart trail. It was well-traveled but not really what a road would be like.

Guiermo spoke, "This likely leads to a farm or small village. Either way we should avoid contact if possible!"

"With over a hundred men I would think that would be hard to do," I said. A moment later a foot patrol of Spanish soldiers came around a curve. The battle was immediate. The soldiers were ready and fired almost before we saw them. We instantly pushed into the brush. Leaving at least three men lying in the trail. I looked around. Vincent was on my right between the brush and me, and Guiermo was on my left. I could hear movement all around.

"This is Left Tenant Jimenez! Your fight is useless. No need to die today! Just give up, and we will escort you to El Morro," came a voice.

Vincent looked at me and put a finger up to his puckered lips meaning to stay quiet. He then motioned for me to stay. He crawled away on all fours. I couldn't hear him move, and he was gone in a second. Where Guiermo went, I had no clue.

From beneath a bush, I plucked a small limb, careful to choose a limb that the white stub would not be seen. I wiped the sandy ground where I left my tracks. I eased beneath a bush that had a thick overhang. I heard, not too far ahead of me, the sudden clash of swords and pistol shots. I heard the angry yells and the painful screams of men realizing they were dying in horrible agony. I had an urge to join the fight, and at the same time I was content to stay where I was. After all I had been told to stay and hide.

The sounds suddenly stopped.

When the soldiers came around the curve and opened fire, Guiermo dove to his left on the opposite side of the trail from Ramon and instantly vanished. He wasted no time in moving in the direction of the solders. There were several men that followed Guiermo. Each one with a sword in their strong hand and a pistol in the other. The left tenant yelling his command to *give up* gave Guiermo a focus point. Guiermo and the men who followed attacked from the left. Vincent and the men who followed him attacked from the right. Vincent and Guiermo both shot simultaneously. Their led balls struck the left tenant in the mid-section, and he dropped without a sound. The battle was fierce and short. The Spaniards put up a fierce fight. Several of the crew were dead. Only the number of men attacking the soldiers won the fight.

Vincent looked at Guiermo. "That will surely bring more soldiers. We need to move now!" he said.

I was under the brush for what seemed like hours. No sounds. The smell of gunpowder was gone. I started to hear a sound. I couldn't tell what it was, but it was very loud and very close. I saw it! A small green frog on a tree. I lie there watching the frog and wandering where the others had gone. *Is Vincent dead? Are they all dead?* I eased out from beneath the brush and looked around. *This place is beautiful.* I began easing my way towards where the battle had taken place. A large green iguana darted across the trail. I came upon the battle scene. I looked around and didn't see Vincent or Guiermo among the dead. All the weapons had been confiscated.

Their tracks in the sandy trail suggested they were running. I assumed towards something. I continued to move forward on the trail. At times I could see the ocean, and sometimes I could not. I decided I would continue walking and following the trail even if it got dark.

It got dark!

CHAPTER VIII

ENLIGHTENMENT

I moved along quietly and began to smell something cooking. I had not eaten anything since the previous evening. The trail split and I went towards the smell. I came upon a small house of very poor construction. I sat down by a palm tree and leaned back against it. I could see a woman in the back cooking on the same kind of estufa my mother cooked on. I sat there watching the woman cook and thinking about my mother and sister, Rena. *How long have I been gone? I was stupid! A real man of the house would have stayed home and be the man of the house!*

I was lost in thought and hunger. Suddenly I felt something cold and thin, against my throat. I froze!

"Now there's a good boy. Are you friend or foe? You're not a friend. I have never seen you," came a voice.

"Please," I said. "I mean you no harm. I can smell your food cooking…" The knife pressed a little harder. Enough that I caught my breath…

"Our food!"

"What?"

"Our food. Me and my family!"

Just then I realized the voice was that of a female, and what sounded like a young female. The knife was no joke. Young or not, I was up against a tree, sitting on the ground. I was at a disadvantage.

"Please! If I could just get a piece of bread."

"You're from that pirate ship that landed this morning! Don't deny it! I have been following you since you left your ship!"

Who is this? "Ma'am, I'm no pirate. Neither are the men I came with. We came to liberate Puerto Rico from the Spaniard rule and free the slaves." Then I realized just how dumb that sounded.

The pressure on the blade let up, then moved away completely. "May I stand up?" I asked as I was standing up slowly with my hands outstretched. "See. No weapons." I slowly turned. There in front of me was a beautiful palm tree. I looked around then turned back towards the house. A girl was standing in front of me with a knife in her hand just inches from my chest.

"How did you do that?" came the words from my mouth. Even in the dark I could see her white teeth smiling.

"Come along. I will see you are fed before you leave."

We entered the cooking area, and there was a dark-haired woman. I guessed to be around my own mother's age. "Look what I brought home!" the girl said while laughing.

The woman looked up sharply. She looked at me then at the girl, "That's the best you can do Nanci? A ragged, skinny boy?"

"He's from that pirate ship. I followed them from their ship all the way to where they fought with the Spanish soldiers."

The lady looked at me with raised eyebrows. "You fought with the soldiers?"

Before I could answer Nanci said, "Not this one! He crawled underneath a bush and stayed there until the fighting was over, and everyone else had left."

"Now to my defense! I did what I was told to do," I exclaimed! The lady handed me a tin plate and spoon. The plate was filled with beans, plantain, and a piece of bread.

"My name is Ana Mari. This is my daughter, Nanci. Sit down and tell us about you," said the lady.

As I ate, I told them of the plan and past battles we had at sea, not leaving out the battle where I killed the two men in the captain's quarter. Finally, I told them of hoping to free my father from the Turkish prison.

"So you're on a quest?" asked Nanci.

"I suppose you could say that. I'm not really sure how long I have been gone. I think maybe close to a year. It was just after the rainy season, and it's almost that time again.

I sometimes think I'm being foolish. My mother and sister are by themselves. Although we have neighbors who will watch out for them, I know they must be worried."

We talked late into the night. Ana brought us coffee with sugar and milk. She sat with us under the stars. Talking about Puerto Rico and the many nations that have ruled over her. She talked about the Indians who were made slaves in their own land.

"Did you know that a Puerto Rican man and women who appear to be Hispanic can have children that appear to have different fathers of different races?" asked Ana.

I was astonished and started to laugh. "Don't laugh. I'm serious. I know a family with three children. The husband and wife are very much in love. They have two boys and one girl. The two boys have their father's features, but one appears black and the other Hispanic. The daughter has blonde hair and blue eyes with her mother's features. That's because there have been many races of people that have intermarried and now their bloodlines have mingled. Sometimes they are different from their parents, but they are all beautiful."

"Wow! That's amazing." I looked at Nanci. "I suppose what you say is true. One thing I know is true! Your daughter is beautiful!" I could not believe I just said that to her mother.

Nanci looked down at the ground, "I don't think I am!"

I could see she was pleased. Ana stood up, looked down at me, and said, "I'm glad you think so. She is sixteen and should be married by now." She turned away and walked back into the house.

We talked. It seemed like forever. I woke the next morning leaning against a palm tree. The birds were singing and the little green frogs were happy. I shook off the sleepiness. I stood up and looked around. Nanci's house seemed even smaller in the daylight. I could see smoke rising from the cooking area. I walked to where Ana was cooking breakfast. She smiled as she asked, "Do young men sleep so long where you are from? I think Nanci wants to take you to one of her favorite places today."

"I'm sure I should go look for the crew."

"Nonsense! They will find you when it's time. If you go wandering around the soldiers will find you. Even though you look like us your Spanish is different. They will know when you talk. They will lock you up in El Morro. Whatever you do, don't talk too much to other people. Not everyone is friendly." She handed me a plate with beans and plantain. I was grateful to get it.

While I was eating, Nanci came out of the house. I almost dropped my plate. Last night I had no trouble telling her she was beautiful. Today when I looked at her in the daylight, I couldn't find words that would come out. I looked at her mom. She gave me a huge smile full of pretty white teeth.

"You're going to have a great day," she said.

"Good morning," said Nancy. "You fell asleep and looked like you really needed it."

"Yes! I guess I was pretty tired."

While Nanci ate, we talked more about Puerto Rico and made plans for the day. We told her mother we would be back before noon and with that, we started walking towards the mountain behind her house. We came to a steep cliff. Nanci pointed up, "We're going up there."

"How?"

Nanci smiled, "Follow me!"

We walked to a small tree that was snug against the cliff face. Nancy grabbed the first branch and pulled herself up. Grabbed another and climbed up the tree.

I was looking up at her and was very pleased. About half the way up the tree she looked down. "A gentleman would not be looking at my ass," she said with a smile.

"I'm no gentleman! I'm a pirate. Remember!"

She smiled back, "Should I be afraid?"

"Not at all."

Nanci sprung over to a ledge, "Up here."

I climbed up the tree and jumped over to the ledge. Nanci was following the ledge up a steep incline. I followed her, stopping every now and then to look around. We were above the treetops now. I could see little streams of smoke rising from the palm trees where there were houses.

Still, we climbed higher and higher. Finally, we reached the top where it was flat, covered in fan bushes and smaller types of trees. We walked along the top until it opened up to a wide flat rock. The view was amazing! The valley below was covered in jungle and at the end of the valley was the ocean. Neither of us said anything for a while. We just sat there taking in the beauty.

"This is not even my favorite place. Come. I'll show you."

We walked back the way we came but continued along the top until we came to the opposite end. We made our way back down to the jungle floor and walked for a short distance. Suddenly Nanci stopped and pointed, "There! That's where we're going."

I could see a tall cliff with trees scattered about. *That's pretty, but what is so great about that? I was thinking to myself.* Suddenly in front of me, there was a waterfall about an arm's length wide that silently cascaded down into a crystal-clear pool.

I turned to express my amazement. Before I could say anything, Nanci placed her hands on my face and pressed her lips to mine. My whole world seemed to fade away and when it came back nothing was the same. "Wow, that was… Can we do that again?

She smiled, "Of course!" and shoved me backward into the pool. I gasped. The water was cold but I soon forgot all about the water because Nanci had stripped down to a thin white shirt and nothing else. The afternoon passed away too quickly. I suddenly found myself more concerned that the crew would come back. I had kissed a girl but never dreamed I would be swimming in such a beautiful place, with a girl that was even more beautiful and not at all shy.

The next two weeks were unbelievable. I woke early and stayed up late talking with Nanci and her mother. I had almost forgotten I was supposed to be a part of a war party. Nanci and I had taken to walking along the beach in the evening. We held hands, and we stopped to kiss every time we thought no one was looking. It was almost dark. The sun was setting in the west. A bold, gold sun surrounded by a blue sky. I could see a star just coming into view. I stood facing the west. Nanci stood facing me. We held each other tight. Nanci began to kiss me, my head turned northward a little. I opened my eyes. *The Bella Donna!*

I suddenly broke off the kiss and held Nanci at arm's length. "What?" she was confused.

I pointed to the ship, "Quick! We must not be seen." We ran back to the house almost too dark to be running. We ran into the back area where we knew Ana would be cooking.

"What is wrong," she asked.

"The *Bella Donna* has returned. That means my time here is short."

Two weeks had passed since I had seen any of the crew that I came to shore with. I had begun to think them all killed or captured. Nanci and I had spent nearly all of our waking moments together during those two weeks. Something had changed in me, and it was due to her. Suddenly I was torn apart. Do I return to the *Bella Donna* or stay with Nanci? It should not have taken more than a passing thought to make that decision. I had kissed a girl before. The first kiss with Nanci changed something inside. Now this was a very difficult decision.

It was full darkness now. I did not eat. I sat beneath the same palm tree where Nanci had held a knife to my throat. Tonight, she had not come to sit with me. I had no idea where she went. She abruptly left shortly after we returned from the beach.

I sat there looking up at the stars and remembering my father and me sitting beneath the Guanacaste tree and the proud feeling I had when I looked up at him. My decision was made. *Family first!*

"May I sit with you a moment, Ramon?"

I looked up at Ana. Though I couldn't see her plainly, I knew she was concerned. I stood quickly, out of respect, "Absolutely! I would be honored for you to sit with me." Nimbly she sat down on the sand. I remained standing for a moment, unsure of what to do. I sat down beside her.

"Nanci is upset. She thought for sure you would stay. I was hoping you would also. I have seen a big change in Nanci since you came here. She tends to be more ladylike."

"I'm so…"

"I'm not finished. I have watched you watch her. I see two young, beautiful people in love. Can you deny it?"

"Ma'am! I don't know what I feel. I need to go with the *Bella Donna* to rescue my father. But it almost hurts inside at the thought of leaving Nanci and never seeing her again."

"May I suggest something? Go find your father, and if you survive, come back here."

"I must discuss this with Nanci," I said.

Ana stood up and for the first time she touched me. She put her hand on my shoulder and said, "You are a fine young man and must come from a strong mother. She raised a gentleman."

Ana turned and walked back to the house. The proposal was made since, but there were a lot of things that could happen. Killed in battle. The captain might not want to come back here. Nanci might have another man before I can get back.

Suddenly there was a knife at my throat. *I hope that's Nanci,* I thought.

"So! This is how we started our trip in this life. How shall that trip end?""

It is Nanci! How does she do that? Suddenly the words came from nowhere. "I love you! I will return. I promise!"

The knife left my throat, and Nanci spun me around. She put the tip of the knife under my chin, "If you do not! I will hunt down the *Bella Donna* and…" I grabbed her and pressed my lips against hers.

"I will be back! I don't know how long it will take but there better not be another man kissing these lips when I return, or you will see a Ramon you have not seen before, and the man will have breathed his last breath."

Nanci gave a little laugh, "He would die with a smile!"

The next morning the three of us walked down to the beach. There was a longboat and beside it was Captain Gaza, Guiermo, and Vincent. I was thrilled to see them.

"I thought we would wait all day for you to show," said Captain Gaza. "After I saw such a beautiful young lady you were with yesterday. I saw you threw the monoscope."

Nanci had dropped back a step or two.

"I think her mother is quite beautiful as well," said the captain.

"Sir! May I speak with you in private," asked Ana.

The two stepped off down the beach away from eager ears and talked. When they returned the captain looked at Nanci, "I promise to bring him back."

As the *Bella Donna* was making way east by northeast, I stood on the aft of the fortress deck and marveled at the beauty of Puerto Rico and the beautiful Nanci Leona Joynes. *I will see you again, Nanci the knife. You didn't cut my throat, but you sliced my heart.*

I stood and watched through the spyglass. I saw Anna give Nanci a hug. I lowered the glass. When I looked again, they were gone.

Nanci stood on the beach long after, watching the *Bella Donna* making way until the sails were almost out of sight. A tear came to her eye. She held her mother's hand, "Will he come back?"

"Hell, nor hurricane will stop him from coming back for you." Anna gave her daughter a hug and they disappeared from the beach.

CHAPTER IX

RAIS HAMIDOU

We had been two days sailing without seeing as much as a bird. Captain Gaza was unusually quiet. He spent a lot of time staring at maps and writing things down. It was obvious we had lost a lot of the crew. Vincent said the battle was furious and unsuccessful. He said the Spanish soldiers were fierce fighters and better equipped. I thought almost every minute about Nanci. It became almost frustrating. I spoke with Vincent about it. I expected him to laugh, but he didn't.

"I will tell you from my experience for I'm not a wise man. Neither a man nor a woman can help who they fall in love with. Once the two meet, something inside tells the woman this is the man that will provide for me and father my children.

The man, on the other hand, may be slow to recognize the behavior from the woman indicating those feelings. If this happens for too long the woman will move on. If by chance, a kiss is exchanged something inside that woman will confirm yes! This is the man for me, and then the man is almost helpless after that first kiss."

I listened to Vincent for what seemed like an hour. "Okay. You have told me a lot about women. I have kissed a girl before and nothing happened other than I was happy I had kissed a girl. But this time was different."

"That is what I have been attempting to help you understand. You cannot control love, my little friend." Vincent placed his big black hand on my shoulder. "She will always be with you even if you never see her again."

"Never see her again? I will see her again if I must sail the *Bella Donna* by myself. I will see her again!"

Nearly a month had passed since leaving Puerto Rico. I was asleep in my hammock when Captain Gaza touched my shoulder. "Ramon, don't make a sound. Go below and tell Vincent and Guiermo to wake everyone as quietly as possible. Remember no sounds!"

It was pitch black outside. There was not a light on the ship anywhere. I walked as quietly and as fast as I could.

I decided to awaken Guiermo first because I knew what can happen if you startle Vincent. It would be noisy indeed. Everyone usually just let him sleep and awaken on his own. I explained to Guiermo the captain stressed no sounds at all. I returned to the captain's quarters.

I didn't say anything. The captain sat at his table with pistol and sword. First Mate Goma was there as well. Even without light from a lantern there is enough natural light that your eyes adjust. I sat down wanting to ask what was going on but dared not to speak. Guiermo and Vincent entered quietly.

In a very soft voice, the captain spoke, "And the crew?"

Vincent replied, "What we have left, sir! The crew is assembled with their weapons on the deck. Everyone is sitting so as not to make an accidental noise."

The captain leaned into the center of the table. "There is a square-rigged ship approximately a mile from here. The wind is calm. Noise and light will carry across the water. We must be prepared for an attack. We will attempt a surprise attack at first light."

Goma spoke, "Sir, we have no wind!"

"We will row, slowly and as quietly as possible. Have the oars wrapped in the cloth where they pass through the porthole. They are to our south and east. We will take them from their aft before they have time to hoist sail."

Vincent spoke, "Who are they? English does not have square rigging?"

"They are Barbary corsairs. Slave traders. They are no doubt on the hunt. They do not care for what's in the hold. They want the men for slaves to be sold in Algiers. We have two advantages. They don't want us dead, and they will not know we are attacking until the first shot from our cannons. All twenty!"

Left tenant spoke again, "How would you like the first rounds, sir?"

"Bolos! Balls and link. I want the first rounds to be as devastating as possible. I want this to end quickly. We don't know if there are more ships that can come to their aid. It is just after midnight. We have a lot of preparation and a mile or more to grow. Let's get it done men."

After everyone left, I asked the captain, "This is what happened to my father?"

Though I could not see his face clearly, for there was no light, I could see he was most sincere, "Very similar to this, only we were the ones caught unaware. The shoe is on the other foot this time."

I walked to the foredeck and stood just behind the bowsprit. I listened but couldn't hear the ores in the water. The *Bella Donna* was moving but without the white water churned up by the bow. Just slow and easy, but yet a good clip.

"Are you sure," asked Rais Hamidou, captain of the *Zebeck* called White Horse, an Algerian-made ship. This ship was a slave ship. A huntress. This captain was famous and throughout his carrier, he will eventually capture more than 200 ships. This ship could hold as many as 400 men. But this one had far less because Captain Hamidou wanted room for a couple of hundred slaves to sail to Algiers and the Ottoman empire.

The sailor stiffened his back, "I'm sure Rais. In the fading sunset, I saw the white sails of what appeared to be an English or perhaps a Spanish ship."

"Or perhaps a French ship! You saw no banners?" asked the captain.

"It was too far away. At first, I thought it was a cloud near the horizon. Then through the haze of sun and water, it seemed to disappear and return. It was headed north."

"Full sail north by west," said the captain. "If we can close the gap, we can determine if she is worthy of taking."

The *Zebeck* sailed into the midnight hours and no sign of the ship. "Lower the sails, and lay anchor," Hamidou commanded.

The crew responded. After all was still, the crew settled down. The thirty-four English slaves in their hold made no sound. These men had heard of what happened to the men captured by Barbary privateers. They were men taken from an English ship and knew they would never see home again.

Early the next morning the crew was gathered on the main deck as was their custom. Every man was on bended knees facing east. As the sun rose a man, considered a holy man, began his morning prayer song. He was loud and beautiful. The crew performed their prayer.

Twenty guns suddenly bellowed as one as the *Bella Donna* fired her cannons, then they fired at will. The first volley was loaded with what Captain Gaza called bolos. They were two cannonballs linked together with a chain and fired as one. The two cannonballs spread a part in flite with the chain still attached. The effect was it would cut anything in its path in two, man or timber.

The *Zebeck* exploded into splinters. The masts and timbers cut to splinters, toppled to the water and onto the praying men. It was so sudden they didn't have a chance to escape the flying shards of wood. The majority of the men died in their spot, on bended knees. There was only a hand full of the privateers remaining alive and the majority of them were injured or dying.

CHAPTER X

EARLY-MORNING SURPRISE

The *Bella Donna* moved with ease in the darkness. The watchmen had spotted the *Zebeck* just before dark. They crept up on the ship slow and steady with the current and just enough manpower to enable steering. Not a single light was on board not even to light a pipe. The *Zebeck* had come to a halt and anchored.

Captain Gaza motioned for First Mate Goma and Guiermo to come to him. "These are Barbary privateers. Slave traders! Kidnapers of man, women, and child. They are religious men called Muslims. They will pray at first light when the sun starts to rise. They will be vulnerable. We must be close enough to fire our cannons with the bolos. All twenty cannons at the same time. The damage will be great enough. It will immobilize the ship before they can retaliate. We will then move in to take the ship."

"If they are holy men, why should we kill them?" asked Guiermo.

"Because if we don't, they will capture everyone. They won't kill the rest of us," replied Goma.

Guiermo looked at the captain, "That doesn't seem very holy to me."

The captain looked at Guiermo, "Not all Muslims are this way. Most are not. These men see their way of life as work. A way to make means for their family."

"That's fine! A slave is a slave."

The *Bella Donna* came to a halt. The *Zebeck* kept a lantern lit on all three of her masts. The *Bella Donna* sat just out of sight of the *Zebeck* in complete darkness. It's a natural thing for a man to look at a light at night. When he looks away his eyesight is diminished, and one can hardly see past the glow of the light.

The night drifted by slowly and yet too fast for me. Guiermo told me of the plan. Actually, he told everyone. "It doesn't seem right to attack them while they pray," I protested.

"It may be the best chance we have, Ramon. That ship can hold as many as four hundred men. It has two times the number of cannons. She is a huntress, and what she doesn't kill she will sell into slavery. If we are captured, I will kill myself before they take me."

I sat on my perch on the bow and watched the *Zebeck*. *How big is this world? We have sailed for over a month. I've never heard of Muslims, Ottoman, and Algiers. The captain said the Ottoman empire had been raiding English and French ships and raiding their villages for over three hundred years and selling the captives into slavery. I'd heard of "Caribes," the African slaves that escaped by force or shipwreck in the Caribbean. The Caribbean islands were full of them. The captain said where we were going was on the edge of another sea called the Mediterranean. How big is this world?*

Such were my thoughts when the captain walked up to me. "It won't be long now, Ramon. These are the same privateers that took your father. They would have had me too but believed me to be dead and left me drifting alone in the ocean with thirty-two men who were dead. I don't mean these are the same individuals, but they come from the same ports. When we board her, I want you to stay aboard and keep control of my quarters. You've done it before, and I trust you more than anyone else. Arm yourself, and be ready for anything. Now go and prepare your fortress! We are about to fire on the *Zebeck* and send her to whoever she prays to."

Suddenly I didn't feel so bad about what was to take place. I went quietly and hastily to the captain's quarters. I knew where every weapon was and could load a pistol or coachmen in the dark. I set about to do just that but found all the weapons were already loaded and primed for action. I sat down in the captain's chair and waited. I noticed the room was getting a little lighter. Suddenly I heard the voice of a man that sounded almost like singing.

I couldn't understand anything but knew this was the prayer time around which the captain had been planning his attack.

The *Bella Donna* shuttered and roared at the same time. She shook so hard I thought she was exploding. The twenty cannons did their work.

Aboard the *Zebeck* men were cut in two by the bolos. Smashed by falling timber and riddled with large and small pieces of wood that had once been rail and rigging. There were men wailing in agony. There was not anyone walking above deck on their own two feet. The *Bella Donna* moved up on the port side and grappling hooks were thrown and secured. There was no resistance, not even a pistol shot.

Captain Gaza was the first one onto the *Zebeck*. He was ready for battle, but there was no one to battle. Leaning against a door was a man still alive but not in any condition to fight. He glared at Captain Gaza, "Who are you to take my ship so effortlessly?"

"I am Captain Luis De Gaza." The captain took a step closer and kicked away a pistol lying too close for comfort to the man. "Who are you?"

"My name is not important. I have not much time left. I am the captain of this ship, but there are others. My name is Rais Hamidou. I would do terrible things to a captain who lost one of my ships, and now I have lost my own."

"How is it you speak our language?"

"I once captured a ship and there was a man, a fierce fighter named…"

"Reynaldo Molina," said Captain Gaza.

"Yes, how did you know?"

"Where can I find Reynaldo?" The captain was apparently growing irritated with Hamidou.

Rais Hamidou glared at the captain and clenched his mouth shut.

Captain Gaza knelt down on one knee. "Do you think I don't know the things you have done? You have ruined more lives than you can believe. When people speak your name, they tremble in fear. The day of reckoning has come to you, my friend! The one thing that will save your life is knowing the whereabouts of Reynaldo Molina." Gaza touched him on his ribs, and the man winced in pain.

"My surgeon can mend you."

Hamidou shook his head violently. "No, you are unclean in the eyes of my god. Don't touch me."

Guiermo walked up to Captain Gaza. "Captain, there are thirty-two English captives in the hold. Everyone else has been dispatched."

Captain Gaza touched Hamidou on the ribs again, just a little bit harder. Hamidou moaned in pain.

"Suffer, you son of a bitch? You don't know pain yet! This ship has been in the water for years. What do you suppose is on the bottom of her belly?"

Hamidou grew a little paler.

"You thought you were the only one to think of that torture?" The captain walked off towards the hold.

I looked at Guiermo, "What's under the ship?" I whispered.

"Barnacles," he replied. A rope will be tied to his hands and another to his legs. He will be thrown overboard on one side of the ship and drug beneath the ship. The barnacles will peel his skin right off of his body."

I looked at Hamidou. He had overheard the conversation. He began to say a prayer of some kind. I couldn't understand his language, but I knew he was praying.

Suddenly a bucket of salty seawater was thrown on Hamidou. "What was that for?" I found myself asking. The sailor looked at me. "He needs to be cleaned up, and he doesn't want us touching him."

It was obvious the seawater was burning the open wounds. Another man came forward with a big smile on his face. "No, you don't," I said. The man froze looking at me angrily. "Boy," he said. "Step out of the way or I'll…"

"You will what?" asked Vincent. The man sat the pale of sea water down and walked away. "This is the captain's prize! No one will harm him further until ordered by the captain!"

The crowd dispersed and set about seeking what could be used on the *Bella Donna*, or for personal gain. The wealth, if any would be put together and distributed as evenly as possible. There was quite a bit that was of value. The men were laughing and gesturing and having a good time. Elated at the wealth they had found. Apparently, this captain had been hoarding wealth for a long time and not just turning it over to the Algerian elite rulers.

Captain Gaza came back on the deck followed by thirty-two happy English sailors. "Make it quick," said Captain Gaza. We need to be underway. We don't know if there are more ships coming to aid. Be quick!" He pointed at Hamidou, "Pick him up, and take him with us." The captain looked at Hamidou, "He doesn't have a choice."

First Mate Goma asked the captain, "What about the ship and the dead?"

Captain Gaza replied, "Let it drift!"

The *Bella Donna* was in full sail and clipping along for a while before I decided I would go to talk with Captain Gaza. I went to the captain's quarters and asked for permission to enter. The Algerian captain was in the cell in pain or sulking, I couldn't decide. "May I speak to the captain?"

"Him or me? " Captain Gaza asked.

"Him, sir!"

Captain Gaza stood, "Do you wish to be alone?"

"Alone? No, sir!"

Captain Gaza puckered up his lips as if thinking hard. He arched an eyebrow, "Do you have a weapon?"

I was taken back a little. *Why in the world would he ask that?* "No, sir! No weapons."

Captain Gaza looked at Hamidou. "This young man has killed several men not far from where you are."

Hamidou looked at me a little differently.

Captain Gaza walked over and patted me around my waist. "No! No weapon. If you wish you may speak with the prisoner." Captain Gaza returned to the table and sat in his chair.

I pulled a chair closer to Hamidou, careful not to get too close.

I was about to speak when Hamidou raised his hand in objection, "I am a captain! You must ask my permission to be spoken to."

"You are a prisoner, and a poor sight of one at that," I replied. I looked at Captain Gaza and saw him smile just a little.

Hamidou sat a little straighter in his hammock. "Forgive me. You are correct. I'm a prisoner. I will speak with you if you allow it."

"Allow it? You are still a man. Talk if you will, but you don't have to!"

Captain Gaza let out a sigh, "Talk already!"

"You said you knew my father."

Hamidou moved his head forward, "I said that?"

"Yes! Reynaldo Molina is my father. I'm here to bring him back or kill him."

"Hey now!" exclaimed Captain Gaza.

Hamidou relaxed back into the hammock, "Your father is a great man even among the Barbary corsairs. When your father was taken, I was among the crew who took him. He killed many of the crew single-handedly. When we finally subdued him, he was covered from head to toe in blood and not a single scratch on him." Hamidou spoke of the event with pride. "Yes, indeed. I know your father! It will be my honor to bring him to you personally."

Captain Gaza slapped the tabletop with the palm of his hand, "That my friend just saved your life! I too have heard of you. I too was on that ship and left for dead. If you will help us, find Reynaldo, my friend and his father. I will not only let you live, but I will also pay you my share of the bounty taken from your ship!"

"Pay me with my own riches?" Hamidou began to laugh, although he grimaced from the pain. "Okay! We have an accord. Tell me. Why did you come all this way for one man?"

CHAPTER XI

THE RESCUE

Captain Gaza was silent for a minute. "I love a good adventure, and this one is worthy. We may yet meet our death. I only recently found out my friend is alive, or I would have been back for him years ago."

Hamidou looked at me "You said you are going to kill him. The captain wishes to save him, and his son wishes to kill him." He smiled. "This may become very interesting."

"I didn't say I wish to kill him, but if he refuses to come with us, I will."

Without releasing Hamidou from the cell, Captain Gaza and he looked over maps and made a planned route to a place called Kaffa, North Africa.

"This place is well fortified and very protective of their income," exclaimed Hamidou. "We will need to make a plan that will allow us access to the port. Your friend works with the bookkeeping and will be close. We need to get him onto the ship and then leave quickly."

We came into port in mid-morning. Hamidou was standing on the bow. The captain was next to him on his left and sat on a crate. Sitting down made the situation seem more relaxed. We bore banners of Dutch affiliation. The Dutch traded slaves here and were common to the watchful eyes.

The plan had been laid. Hamidou would go to the harbor office where Reynaldo would be working. I was to go with him since he had not seen me since I was five years old. He would not recognize me, and it insured Hamidou would not betray us. I had a pistol in my waistband and a knife tucked behind my back. Captain Gaza gave me the weapons in front of Hamidou. "If he decides to betray us, don't hesitate to shoot him." He positioned me behind Hamidou just to his left, "Walk just like this the entire time." Captain Gaza said all of this while looking straight into the eyes of Hamidou.

Hamidou was to tell the authorities that he had something on board of value and wants Reynaldo to evaluate its worth. The thirty-two English sailors who had been enslaved would be standing on the deck in full view holding ropes in their hands as if tied together. Hamidou was a well-known privateer and would be welcomed without question.

That was the plan. We had gotten lucky coming across the *Zebeck*. Otherwise, we would never have been able to fight our way in and out of that harbor.

We entered the harbor slowly. Hamidou looked at Captain Gaza, "I will never be able to return to this port after this day. I will be beheaded on site."

"There are plenty of ports who deal in the slave trade," said Gaza.

We came close to the main pier. Using the ores, we turned facing out to sea. There was no wind or tide, so the anchor was dropped. But it was an anchor that would never hold in wind or current. It was intentionally used because we could cut the rope and leave quickly using the oars while the sails were hoisted. The entire *Bella Donna* crew was either on an oar or manning the cannons.

Hamidou and I climbed down the Jacob's ladder and into a longboat with two crew members manning the oars. They were unarmed so as not to present a threat. Hamidou was also unarmed as was the custom. Only I had weapons and they were out of sight. I sat just behind and to the left of Hamidou. In a quiet voice he said, "Ramon, you make me nervous."

"Don't worry! I will make it quick. You won't feel a thing."

Hamidou laughed out loud, "That is very thoughtful of you, Ramon."

We climbed from the longboat onto the pier. The two crewmen stayed with the boat. Hamidou and I walked towards the Harbor office. I walked just as the captain had shown me. Our footsteps were loud and hollow as if trying to tell me something.

There were piles of skins, and something called ivory tusks. There were bundles of silk and fabrics of all colors. The place was overwhelming. I had never seen most of the things I was looking at and so can't describe them.

I was suddenly very nervous. I was nearly shaking. *I'm about to see my father for the first time since I was five years of age. I cannot let on I know him. Don't say anything. Don't even look at him. Don't say anything at all.*

Hamidou and I reached the front door of the office. It was huge. Made from stone. There were six guards and at least one small canon on the roof. Suddenly one of the guards smiled big. "Hamidou! Where is your ship? Did you lose it?" The other guards laughed.

"It will be here tomorrow. I took this one two days ago."

The door opened and a fat, short man looked at Hamidou, "What is your business today?"

Hamidou used his head and nodded towards the *Bella Donna*. "I took her yesterday."

"You don't usually bring the ship, only the crew. What's different about this one and where is your *Zebeck*?" The questions seemed harmless, yet I felt he was suspicious.

He knows something isn't correct. If anything happens shoot him and run like the wind, zigging and zagging.

"Everyone is full of jokes today, Abou!" said Hamidou.

"It's okay. Come on inside. Let's talk business."

We entered the room, and my eyes had to adjust from the bright sun to the darkroom.

Captain Gaza sat back in his room with a spyglass. Guiermo and two other men had their long guns trained on the guards on top of the roof.

On the *Bella Donna* Captain Gaza was watching closely with his spyglass. "They seem to be friendly. The guards are laughing." Captain Gaza was giving moment-by-moment updates.

Below deck twenty cannons were loaded, each one with a target. The targets were guard towers and cannon placements. Too many to cover them all. This place was built and added too for hundreds of years. It would take an attack by land and sea to take this place.

"They went inside. Nothing to do but wait. Keep your target, and be ready," said Captain Gaza.

The room was cool inside. There were tables with bags of money and stacks of papers. Behind one of the desks sat a man with long dark hair and broad shoulders who was busy writing on papers and stamping them.

It was all I could do to keep from yelling out *"Father!"* and running to him as fast as I could. My head was starting to swim.

What if Hamidou betrays us? I'm the only one here. Escape would be impossible. I will kill him if he betrays us. Die or not, he will die before I do.

Suddenly Hamidou spoke.

"I have something of value on my new ship, and I would like for Reynaldo to come and evaluate it. I also have thirty-two English sailors to sell. We can bargain a price after he has evaluated the prize." Hamidou wasted no time. He was matter-of-fact, and it was apparent he had done this, many times. I didn't know if I admired the man or hated him. Time would tell. Thinking of all the lives this man had ruined made me angry, but now wasn't the time to be thinking! It was time to be paying attention.

"I would accompany you, but I don't like those longboats, and I'm a terrible swimmer," said Abou.

Reynaldo stood. He wasn't as tall as I remembered him. Average in stature but carried a serious almost sad look on his face. "Come, let's get this done! I don't place a price on humans! If this is a woman or child, don't waste my time."

He began walking towards the door and glanced at me. For a split second he paused, and his forehead wrinkled a little, then he kept going. As we walked, I pushed between Reynaldo and Hamidou. "Excuse me," I said, "It is very important I walk where I was instructed to walk."

Reynaldo spoke, "Hamidou, since when did you keep a young manservant?"

Hamidou laughed, "Only recently. This one is special. He is quite the little killer. Don't let his young appearance fool you. He is a man!"

I could feel the pride swell up in my chest. *He called me a man and said it to my father. I'm walking next to my father.* My arm bumped his. The first time we touched since we talked beneath the Guanacaste tree when he told me of masts and ships.

Captain Gaza spoke up, "They are leaving the building, and all seems to be well. The short man is standing at the door but doesn't seem to be concerned. Hamidou seems to be relaxed. He's laughing. Ramon is walking exactly where he is supposed to be. Beside him is... Reynaldo 'The Judge' Molina. They're getting in the longboat. No one is following. This is crazy. I would never have believed it could be done!"

Guiermo relaxed and laid his rifle down, "I can't believe it! He doesn't have a clue he is being rescued. I only hope he sees it that way. Ten years is a long time. A man might get adjusted and forget his previous life."

The longboat came alongside the *Bella Donna*. Two ropes splashed down, and they were tied to the boat. The men in the longboat climbed up the Jacob's ladder and onto the deck of the *Bella Donna*. All this Abou saw from the door of the office. He turned around went back inside. Had he stayed he would have seen the longboat being hoisted from the water and the ores slide out and began the *Bella Donna* moving.

One of the guards noticed, "Hey! Is he supposed to be leaving? He has Reynaldo!"

"Who knows the business of Hamidou," replied another.

Abou walked to the door, "Hey! He didn't say anything about leaving."

The first man spoke, "He said to us, he wanted Reynaldo to evaluate something on his ship. I guess he meant the *Zebeck*."

Abou stood and watched as the sails unfurled, and the *Bella Donna* picked up speed. "That is one beautiful ship."

When Reynaldo's foot stepped on deck, he looked around and seemed to become sullen.

Hamidou spoke, "Come this way please." He led them to the captain's quarters.

"How did you come to take this ship?" asked Reynaldo.

Hamidou smiled, "I will explain shortly."

The ship gave a jerk as she started moving, "What is this?"

He's not willing to go! My hand went to my pistol. A strong hand grabbed my wrist, and a tear came into my eye. "Easy boy," said Guiermo. "Give him a minute."

"A minute for what?" shouted Reynaldo. "What is going on? Why am I here on the *Bella Donna*?"

Captain Gaza came from the captain's quarters. There was a loud ruffle as the sails caught the wind.

"So, you recognize the ship and not your friends?" asked Captain Gaza.

Reynaldo looked about him, seeming to recognize for the first time just who was here. "Luis De Gaza?" Tears started down his face. "*My* God answers prayers!"

Guiermo cleared his throat, "You don't recognize me? I can understand it's been a while."

"Guiermo…from San German? What in the world are you doing here? Is this real? I'm really here on the *Bella Donna*? With my two best friends sailing away from that hell hole. My God answers prayers!" he exclaimed again. "You hear me, young man?"

"Yes, He does," I said and lunged into my father's arms and squeezed him as hard as I could.

Reynaldo was puzzled, "What?"

Guiermo spoke, "Reynaldo, meet again your son, Ramon."

My father fell to his knees dragging me with him. He couldn't speak. I was so overwhelmed I couldn't speak either. Both of us were so overjoyed nothing else seemed to matter.

Hamidou spoke, "I hate to interrupt. But there is a small village nearby. You can draw close enough that I will take a chance on the sharks and swim to shore." The deal was made, and we watched as Hamidou swam to shore.

It was later the same day my father and I were sitting in my favorite spot, just behind the bowsprit. I was so overwhelmed I couldn't prioritize my feelings. I had accomplished my vow to myself and my mother. I rescued my father, and we were on the way back to San German. There was part of me that wouldn't let go of the girl I left behind in Puerto Rico. I promised Nanci I would return. Hardly a day passed that I wasn't thinking about her.

My father placed his hand on my shoulder. "I can't believe I'm free. My own son rescued me. You are quite the man, Ramon. I wished I could have been there while you were becoming this man that you are!"

I nearly started to cry. Many nights I wondered if he deserted me and his family. Many mornings I sat under the big Guanacaste tree and remembered our last conversation about a ship in the harbor. Now I know the ship was the *Bella Donna*, and we were on her deck right now. Now we were on our way back! I said as much to my father. He squeezed my shoulder and with tears streaming down his face he said, "I love you too, son. More than all the stars in the sky."

In the following days, we fell into our routines. I watched my father work. It seemed he was right at home right here on the *Bella Donna*. Often at night I listened while he and the captain exchanged stories of adventures they had shared and adventures unknown to one another. I was happy to just listen and say nothing. Some stories were just stories but told as if a fact. My favorite was the Sea Witch. It goes like this.

CHAPTER XII

THE SEA WITCH

The winds slashed at the sails. The timbers creaked and moaned. Waves broke over the bow. Daybreak would be coming soon. The ship and crew had been fighting the winds all night. No one was sure the entire crew was still on board. The crew tied themselves to anything that was solid.

"Captain, we're going to flounder," cried the helmsman.

"Keep her into the wind. Be hardy men this will blow over soon!"

As suddenly as the storm struck, it stopped. The waves settled. The men looked about. Checking themselves and one another. Daylight was breaking, and to the relief of the sailors, gulls were crying. A sure sign of land. The ship had sustained minor damage that could be easily repaired.

"Hurray! Hurray for the captain," they began yelling. But the cheers would soon stop. A moan could be heard coming from across the waves. Slowly a tall gray cliff loomed in the distance.

The captain broke out monocular. Peering through the lens the captain saw palm trees. He saw a waterfall flowing from the top of the cliff. On top of the cliff was a castle. A white castle with blue, gray, and red banners. As they grew closer, he could see there were no cannons or turrets.

"Make for the beach lads. She looks peaceful. There is fresh water and fruit," said the captain.

As the ship got closer, the crew could hear a woman's voice singing. They couldn't understand a word, but each sailor felt it was the most beautiful song ever heard. Some began to get teary-eyed. Some became frightened.

A sailor tied himself to the main. "If any man tries to free me, I will cut his throat," he growled.

The captain had nothing to say. Every bone in his body said to turn the ship around. He couldn't murmur a word. The ship seemed to be moving on its own now. Headed for the cliff.

Inside the castle was a beautiful woman dressed in black. Her clothing was worn until it was thin and ragged. She gazed into a gold cauldron full of seawater. Beside her stood a knight in blush green armor. He carried a sword in both hands. Affixed to his armor, on each sleeve was a curved sword. His shoulders were donned with spikes.

"They are getting closer," said the woman. "Come! Come," she repeated over and over. Each time getting louder.

The giant knight moaned. He couldn't speak. He could only fight and moan.

"I will go to the beach and escort them here to the castle. Wait on the balcony."

"*Moan*," came a reply.

"Look!" Cried the sailor on the lookout. "There's a woman in white on the beach." These were the first words uttered since the men heard the singing.

Chatter broke out among the men. Every bone in the captain cried danger. They needed the freshwater. They needed the fruit. They needed time to repair what the storm had damaged.

The helmsman approached the captain, "Where are we? I can't find this on the maps."

"Lower the longboats! Reconvene on the beach!" The captain looked at the helmsman. "Maybe she can tell us." The captain stepped onto Jacob's ladder and disappeared over the side.

There was silence as the men slid the longboats onto the sandy beach. The captain looked about. He noticed the forest was without sound. No birds. No gulls. No breeze.

"It is always quiet after a storm." The captain turned and faced a beautiful lady with well-kept, long black waves of hair flowing over her bare shoulders. "The jungle," she repeated. "It is always quiet after a storm."

"*Oh.* Yes, I'm sure." said the captain. *Something is still wrong!* He thought this but couldn't place what it was.

"I am Lady Decapoda. You may just address me as a madam. I don't expect you to remember the name." She gave a beautiful smile. A sailor nearby named Lucco began to repeat the name "Decapoda, Decapoda, Decapoda," as he walked away. Clearly mesmerized by the beauty of Decapoda.

The lady smiled at the captain again, "I'm sure your men are quite hungry after the long night you must have endured. Why not come up to the castle and rest? Refresh yourselves, and you can work tomorrow." She said this loud enough every man could hear her. To do anything else would have led to a riot and the captain dancing the hempen jig.

Lucco, who was enchanted by the woman heard, "Why don't you come to my room and refresh yourself. I will show you pleasures you never dreamed of."

The crew formed a single line, following Decapoda on a trail through the jungle. The trail went up and up. Huge blue and red birds flew back and forth through the trees.

The captain and crew assembled on the balcony. There was a huge table with chairs enough for everyone. There were white plates not metal pans. Silver forks. Silver goblets filled with wine. There were bowls of fruit such as mangoes, oranges, pineapple, and bananas. Everything you can imagine.

The woman was not there. There was a sudden moan. Everyone turned and faced the door they had entered. A giant of a man stood in the doorway. A knight in full armor. Another moan accompanied by a motion they all took to mean sit. Everyone sat. The knight then walked to the end of the table and stood next to the empty chair.

"Captain? Where is Lucco," asked the helmsman.

"I don't know. The last time I saw him he was walking away repeating the madam's name 'Decapoda,' over and over."

Lucco was trailing behind everyone else leaving the beach. He was still repeating Decapoda to himself. It seemed he couldn't stop. In his mind he wanted to shout to the captain there is something evil here. But not a word came out except Decapoda.

When they entered the castle there was a hallway that went straight ahead. Everyone mounted the stairs except Lucco. He was being pulled down the hallway by an unseen force. The walls seemed to blur, and he was moving more rapidly than was humanly possible. He could not stop.

Two huge doors swung open to an elaborate bedroom. Standing in the center, naked as a newborn baby was Decapoda. Her black flowing hair rested on her bare breast. Lucco was done far. He was utterly helpless. Any resistance he had been trying to muster was gone.

Decapoda held out a hand and motioned for him to come to her. He did. When he reached her, his fingertips touched her outstretched hand. Lucco became a pile of fish flopping around on the floor. Two hags and another creature, part man and part pig, quickly grabbed up the fish and ran off into the kitchen.

Decapoda entered the balcony soon after the knight took his place next to her chair. She was dressed again in all white, with a wreath of plumeria flowers on her head.

"Please everyone, drink! Eat! Your supper will be here shortly. Don't let Anomura scare you. I assure you he is a gentle giant."

The men began to loosen up. The wine was having its effect. Each man took a turn asking questions of Decapoda who answered all questions promptly and almost girlishly.

The cooks arrived. Three lovely ladies pushing carts laden with nicely sized fish.

Each plate had an entire fish lying on a bed of rice with a side of fried plantain and sliced lemon for the fish. Everyone ate their fill and complimented the young ladies on the fine meal, to which they just giggled like young girls.

The captain cleared his throat, "The morning will come early. We should all, I mean all, return to the ship," said the captain.

"Nonsense," said Decapoda. There are beds for everyone. Anomura will show you to the quarters. I wager it has been a long time since you have slept in a bed, instead of a hammock. We will meet here in the morning for breakfast. Then afterward you may feel free to repair your ship."

"Very well," said the captain. "Anomura, if you will be so kind to lead us."

"*Moan*," replied the knight.

The night passed without incident to the men. The beds were comfortable and the men were asleep before their heads hit the pillow. Except for the captain and the helmsman.

The helmsman slithered on his belly over to the captain, afraid of being seen. He didn't know who or if anyone was watching. The hairs on his neck were standing up. He eased up to his knees, "Captain, something isn't right here!"

"A lot isn't right here." replied the captain. "Did you notice there were no noises coming from the jungle? There was no debris from the storm. The big blue and red birds were macaws. They are very noisy birds. They never squawked a single time."

"Where did Lucco go, Captain? No one has seen him."

"Don't sleep tonight! We will keep watch over the men."

The helmsman whispered, "Aye, Captain," and slithered his way back to his bed. The helmsman didn't stay in his bed at all. He slithered on his belly and crawled from the room through a small window that led to the terrace outside. He spotted a dim light coming from inside the castle.

The helmsman crept up to the window and cautiously peered in. There were three hags and a half-man, half-pig creature. The three hags were filling the goblets with something from a black pot. The pig was filling the cups with a clear liquid that was not water. Having seen enough he snuck back to his bed.

The night was long and dark. There were no sounds at all. Finally, daybreak was revealing itself. The room was becoming brighter.

"Wake up, Jacob. Day's breaking," commanded the captain. Every man sprung to his feet at attention. "Everyone, come close!" They obeyed.

The helmsman briefly revealed what he had seen.

The captain stated in a stern voice, "We are in some kind of trouble. I don't know what. Everyman be alert for anything you are not comfortable with."

The captain led the men in a prayer asking God for protection against the seen and unseen. Something men do when they fear death if they believe in God or not.

"Do not drink anything. Pretend if you must but do not drink!" The meeting was cut short when Anomura swung the giant doors open.

"*Moan!*" He turned and the men followed him to the balcony. On the huge table were the silver goblets filled with a liquid. Beside it was a smaller cup. It too was filled with something that appeared to be water. While the men were milling about and Anomura was trying to keep an eye on everyone, simultaneously the helmsman and the captain switched their water and wine for that of Anomura and Decapoda's vessels.

The captain took his place next to where Decapoda would be sitting. Decapoda appeared as beautiful as ever in a sea blue dress that faded to a sea green color.

While still standing, Decapoda announced, "It is a tradition that we toast a new day. We first drink the wine from the glass to signify the night has passed. We then drink the water to signify the purity of the day ahead."

"Shall we toast the wine?"

They all pretended to drink and returned their goblets. Decapoda seemed a little confused and quickly regained her confidence.

"Now, the water. Everyone, toast the day." Decapoda and Anomura drank their water. Everyone pretended to drink theirs. Suddenly Decapoda jumped up from her chair. She wheeled around in anger facing Anomura. "How could you..." her voice trailed she flung herself at

Anomura. He swooped her up in his arms and suddenly they burst into a cloud of smoke. They seemed to have disappeared.

"Look!" Shouted the helmsman. Where they had been standing was a crab. A blue crab. The men gathered around. The captain picked up the angry crab with pinchers snapping. The color of the shell was that of Decapoda's dress. The crab had pinchers favoring the knight's swords and sleeves. His armor was the crab's shell. On the shell, was the outline of the sea witches' dress. The captain placed the crab on the floor. The crab began snapping its pinchers and scuttling backward. The crab fell from the balcony and into the sea below. Still today every blue crab has the dress of the sea witch, imprinted on its shell.

When captain Gaza told the story it was as if he were there and it happened to him.

I looked up at my father. He was deep in thought. No doubt he was thinking of my mom, his wife. We sailed for another month. I didn't think of Nanci as much as I used to. I guess I didn't dwell on her. I still wanted to return and claim her for my wife, if she would have me.

CHAPTER XIII

HOME

We sailed for another month. Once we encountered a Dutch ship that attempted to fight us. The battle was short, and we weren't boarded but left her stranded.

"They get what they deserve," said my father.

"Still judging, I see." said the captain.

Early one morning, First Mate Goma came to my room. I was still in the hammock. "Captain wishes to see you." He turned and walked away.

That was odd for him. He usually exchanged some kind of pleasantry. I went immediately to the captain's quarters. I knocked and he answered from within, also unusual.

The captain was seated at his table. "Sit, Ramon. I would like to speak with you." I sat down and leaned forward a little. "Your father isn't here. He is at the bowsprit. I wanted to ask you if you would consider staying with me after you visit home. I don't intend to keep fighting. I wish to start hauling merchandise from Nassau, Cuba, and Florida to a place called New Orleans. It will be no doubt dangerous but less so than what we have experienced."

"Captain! I…"

"Let me finish, please. I think you will be a fine captain. I wish to take you under my teaching and train you myself. I have spoken with your father, First Mate Goma, and Guiermo. I wish to gain four more vessels and eventually you will captain one of them yourself."

"What of my father?"

"He never wishes to leave San German again. I believe his words were, 'Judge Molina is dead! Farmer Molina took his place.' The captain continued. I will spend a few days in San German. I plan on leaving within a week. I wish to sail to this New Orleans. I hear I can purchase a ship there. I will return, and you can give me your answer. Now go join your father." He smiled, "We are about to enter the harbor of San German."

My blood rushed to my head. Without a word I ran, jumped, and swung on ropes. Whatever I could to reach my father. I joined him at the bowsprit. Tears were flowing down his cheeks, "San German," he said in a whisper. I wrapped both arms around him and held him close.

The *Bella Donna* anchored in the harbor. My father and I, though still excited beyond words, had recomposed. He had nothing to retrieve. I grabbed my swag, and down the Jacob's ladder we went. We nearly ran up the mountain to my house. My father and I walked around to the kitchen where we both knew my mom would be. I stepped around first and was going to say, "Mom, please step away from the fire. I have something to show you." When the word *mom* came from my mouth, she spun around, looked at me less than a second, ran across the kitchen in three steps, and literally picked me up off my feet.

"I can't believe it. My son is home!" she shouted out loud. Just then my father stepped around the corner. My mom turned white and collapsed onto the floor.

I, my father, my mother, and my sister all sat under the Guanacaste tree. My father told his story, and I shared my story including Puerto Rico and Nanci, although I left out various parts of course. We reunited until almost the next morning.

Captain Gaza joined us the next day. Guiermo stopped by and didn't stay long, "I have a home to go to! It may be empty, but I plan to change that soon enough!" He turned and went on up the mountain.

The *Bella Donna* left a week later. Part of me wanted to go. I decided to give it more time. I talked the offer over with my family. It was decided that when the *Bella Donna* returned I would begin my apprenticeship to be captain. As Captain Gaza was getting into the long-boat. I relayed the decision to him. He was happy to hear it. As he was shoving off he said, "When you join me, our first stop will be Puerto Rico. I believe you made a promise to a young lady there!"

That was it. The deal was sealed. My fate? The *Bella Donna*.

I am the captain. I'm standing on the deck of the *Bella Donna*. We are anchored in the small harbor of San German. I can hear the howler monkeys in the jungle beginning their day. I smell the ocean and feel the gentle breeze on my face. I'm waiting for the cargo to be loaded and then I will sail this ship to New Orleans Trade City Port. That's another story.

ABOUT THE AUTHOR

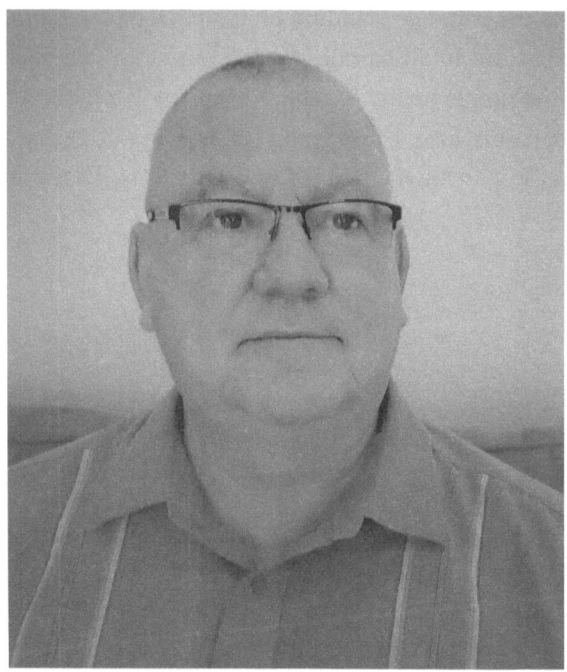

I was born in south Mississippi and grew up on a farm in West Central Mississippi. After college, I lived in Costa Rica, Honduras, and Puerto Rico. A year after the 9/11 attack, I was told to leave Puerto Rico, and I came to Texas. I am now a retired Texas State Trooper. I enjoy writing and incorporate my experiences mixed with historical events and characters to create fiction with tidbits of historical fact. I hope you enjoy the stories, and maybe you will become curious about events and characters and research them. Knowledge goes a long way.